W9-CKB-005

SMALL *Oxford* BOOKS

DUBLIN

SMALL *Oxford* BOOKS

DUBLIN

Compiled by
BENEDICT KIELY

Oxford New York
OXFORD UNIVERSITY PRESS
1983

Oxford University Press, Walton Street, Oxford OX2 6DP

London Glasgow New York Toronto
Delhi Bombay Calcutta Madras Karachi
Kuala Lumpur Singapore Hong Kong Tokyo
Nairobi Dar es Salaam Cape Town
Melbourne Auckland

and associates in
Beirut Berlin Ibadan Mexico City Nicosia

Compilation, introduction, and editorial matter
© *Benedict Kiely 1983*

British Library Cataloguing in Publication Data

Kiely, Benedict
Dublin – (Small Oxford books)
1. Dublin (Dublin) – History
I. Title
941.8'35   DA995.D75
ISBN 0-19-214124-4

Library of Congress Cataloging in Publication Data

Main entry under title:
Dublin.
(Small Oxford books)
Includes index.
1. Literary landmarks—Ireland—Dublin (Dublin)
2. Authors, Irish—Homes and haunts.
3. Dublin (Dublin)—Description—Guide-books.
I. Kiely, Benedict.
PR8731.D8 1983   820'.9'0415   82–12545
ISBN 0-19-214124-4

Set by New Western Printing Ltd.
Printed in Great Britain by
Hazell Watson & Viney Limited
Aylesbury, Bucks

Introduction

Not so long ago I took part in a curious sort of radio programme presented by that wandering man of Irish radio, Donnacha O Dulaing. The other participants were Dr John Cowell, a medical doctor, and the author of a most useful book on the literary past of this city: *Where They Lived in Dublin*. Then there was the librarian of Marsh's library, Dr Muriel McCarthy; and a group of veteran employees of Córas Iompair, Éireann, the Irish Transport Company.

We boarded a number 10 bus at the Phibsboro' gate of the Phoenix Park, close to the splendid Peoples' Gardens and the zoo and the austere building where policemen had been trained in the British days and Gardai, the same thing, from the early 1920s until the training depot was removed to Templemore in County Tipperary. The idea was to follow Route Ten south all the way to the far end of Donnybrook, to the terminus at the radio and television studios and the vast new campus of University College (UCD), and on the way to talk about Dublin.

The programme spilled over into several programmes: what with the scholarship of the doctor and the librarian and the memories of the veterans, and the crowded associations of the city itself. In any old city or, indeed, in any old small town, the earth is layered and its surface cluttered with associations: and more and more I have come to admire, and envy, the order and clarity of the book *The Town* that Leigh Hunt, the Londoner, offered in tribute to his city.

Also, in the company I was in, I was painfully

conscious that I have only been forty-two years in this city (disregarding school holidays before 1940), and that my son who was born here might accept me as a Dubliner but not as a Dublinman: there is a difference.

Our bus-route was by what was once the Cattle Market where the steaming products of the grasslands of Meath changed hands before they (most of them) left for England: then by Doyle's Corner and Mountjoy Jail and the Mater Hospital and the monument to the Four Masters who chronicled ancient Ireland at the time of the Gaelic collapse. To the left there, in Eccles Street, Leopold Bloom set out on his odyssey.

Then by Parnell (Charles Stewart) Square and O'Connell (Daniel) Street, and the General Post Office and 1916, and the place where Nelson used to stand away up there; and Anna Livia Plurabelle and Trinity College, and Nassau Street and Dawson Street and the Green, and Baggot Street and the Grand Canal and Waterloo Road, and Morehampton Road (where did all those English names come from?), and my own front door; and over the Dodder river, and that was that.

But it occurred to me that a few thousand people just could not find room on that bus; long queues of ghosts beckoned from every stop, and at no stop did we stop.

So with the bus journey we are now about to make. We can but begin from where we are and go as far as the bus takes us, and take on just as many or as few as the bus may hold; and if *en route* the bus fails to stop for Johnny Fortycoats, or Love Joy and Peace, or Bang Bang, or a second time for Seán O'Casey or yet another time for Jonathan Swift, or, or, or . . . can I be held in blame? Dublin transport is not what it was in the days of the trams.

B.K.

A STORY

During the Hitler war when transport, with many other matters, was in trouble, a citizen complained bitterly that he was not allowed on to the last bus out of town on a certain route. He had family pride and he said: 'I am one of the Glenns of Kilbarrack and I insist on boarding this bus.'

And the conductor said: 'Sir, if you were one of the Glens of Antrim, I still couldn't fit you in.'

Dubliners and Dublinmen

AN INTRODUCTION TO DUBLIN

Those wickerwork causeways were also often designated by the word *cliath* (clee) which primarily means a hurdle . . . An artificial ford of this kind was constructed across the Liffey in very early ages; and the city that subsequently sprung up around it was from this called *Ath-Cliath* (Ah-clee), the ford of the hurdles which was the ancient name of Dublin. This is the name still used by speakers of Irish in every part of Ireland; but they join it to *Bally : Baile-atha-cliath* (which they pronounce Blaa-clee), the town of the hurdle ford.

The present name, Dublin, is written in the annals: *Duibh-Linn*, which in the ancient Latin life of Saint Kevin is translated *nigra therma*, i.e. blackpool; it was originally the name of that part of the Liffey on which the city is built, and is sufficiently descriptive at the present day. *Duibh-linn* is sounded *Duvlin* or *Divlin*, and it was undoubtedly so pronounced down to a comparatively recent period, by speakers of both English and Irish; for in old English writings, as well as on Danish coins, we find the name written *Divlin*, *Dyflin*, &c., and even yet the Welsh call it *Dulin*. The present name has been formed by the restoration of the aspirated *b* . . .

Patrick Weston Joyce, *The Origin and History of Irish Place Names*, 1869

Gerry O'Flaherty, a young Dublin publisher, in an article in Ireland of the Welcomes *(Jan.–Feb. 1975) said that James Joyce displayed his usual precision of language when he called his famous collection of short stories* Dubliners.

In 1905 Joyce made his statement on the matter in a letter to the London publisher Grant Richards. They were debating the moral British printer's objections to the use of the word 'bloody' in the manuscript of Dubliners. *Joyce wrote*:

I do not think that any writer has yet presented Dublin to the world. It has been a capital of Europe for thousands of years, it is supposed to be the second city of the British Empire and it is nearly three times as big as Venice. Moreover, on account of many circumstances which I cannot detail here, the expression Dubliner seems to me to bear some meaning and I doubt whether the same can be said for such words as 'Londoner' and 'Parisian' both of which have been used by writers as titles. From time to time I see in publishers' lists announcements of books on Irish subjects, so that I think people might be willing to pay for the special odour of corruption which, I hope, floats over my stories.

An arrogant and irritable young man; and, perhaps, at that moment, if not later in life, he might have been confounded by the use of the word Parisienne, *and by the impossibility of finding its equal in relation to Dublin or London : or Oxford itself.*

But here and now is Gerry O'Flaherty's argument :

A Dubliner is an inhabitant of that city who may or may not have been born there, whereas the trueborn native with the city in his blood will always proclaim himself to be a Dublinman.

And furthermore, Mr O'Flaherty continues :

Dublin, in common with most places in the world, has its own slang and peculiar way of using ordinary words . . . The generic Dublinman will address another as Jem, which may be varied to Jemser if the person referred to is not within their hearing: or Jembo, if he is a child. Brendan Behan gaelicized this by calling a character in *The Quare Fellow* Shaybo. People from other parts of Ireland refer to Dubliners as Jackeens or Gurriers. Jackeen in the city, always meant a cunning, loud-mouthed, ignorant youth: while Gurrier was a term of approbation. (One possible derivation: *Guerier*.) In the Thirties and Forties to be a Great Little Gurrier was to be a bosom friend, a fine fellow, a taproom companion: but today it has been debased and is the equivalent of a bowsey or a gouger. A bowsey is usually an unemployed layabout who loves nothing better than to shout abusive remarks, usually of a sexual nature, after passing girls. A gouger is a low ignorant lout who would not hesitate to use physical force when it suited him.

The city dweller's pretence of contempt for a person from rural parts is reflected in such words as Bogman, Bogtrotter, Country Mohawk, the Swiftian Yahoo, or even Baluba which dates to the participation of Irish forces with the UN in the Congo in the 1960s. The term of ultimate abuse for an ignorant person is Culchie. But this, too, was once a term of praise for the fine strong labourers who came from the district around Kiltimagh in County Mayo.

Could it be that the word Culchie may be of more ancient Irish origin and not limited to simple association with the decent town of Kiltimagh? – a name that few Saxons will get right at the first attempt. Edmund Spenser describing the plight of the Irish after the Desmond Wars in the sixteenth century wrote, in that famous or infamous passage in A View of the Present State of Ireland *(1633):*

Out of every corner of the woodes and glinnes they came creeping forthe upon theyr handes, for theyr legges could not beare them; they looked like anatomyes of death, they spake like ghostes crying out of theyr graves; they did eate of the dead carrions, happy were they yf they could finde them . . .

So that town-dwellers and planters as far back as that might have thought of the native Irish, or rural dwellers, as those who came out of the woods : As na Coillte. Culchies ?

Gouger is a corruption of Gauger, or customs and excise man, the evil and official foe of all free spirits who like their spirits free ; and Bowsy was sometimes used in the sense of blackleg or strike-breaker.

In the 1940s the late Francis MacManus, a fine novelist, wrote for the Capuchin Annual *a long essay on Matt Talbot, the saintly and most ascetic Dublin working-man, whose sudden death in Granby Lane near Parnell Square revealed a life of Anthonian self-discipline. When MacManus was enquiring in T. and C. Martin's timber-yard, on the North Wall, of men who had known Matt, he came on one veteran trade-unionist who described him as a 'rejisterred (registered) bowsy'. No reflection on his virtue but on the fact that Matt was so far divorced from the things of this earth as to neglect to pay his union dues.*

Donnybrook

It is a great art to saunter, Thoreau said, and Dublin may still be the golden city for saunterers : it has been said that it is a most excellent city for idlers and retired people.

The saunter can begin anywhere and end anywhere, according to your tastes and your stamina ; but if I had with me at the moment a visitor to the city I'd begin, for

*obvious reasons, right here where I'm writing in Donny-
brook. That is now a select semi-suburb on the south side
of the city and about half an hour's walk from St Stephen's
Green and the top of Grafton Street. But because of a
famous fair held here long ago Donnybrook has given a
word to the American but not, oddly enough, to the
English language as commonly spoken either here or on
the island across the water. The fair was famous or
infamous, nineteenth-century emigrants carried its reputation across the Atlantic and to many Americans a
donnybrook is, quite simply, a rough house:*

To Donnybrook, steer, all you sons of Parnassus,
Poor painters, poor poets, poor newsmen and knaves,
To see what the fun is that all fun surpasses,
The sorrow and sadness of green Erin's slaves.
Oh, Donnybrook, jewel! full of mirth is your quiver,
Where all flock from Dublin to gape and to stare
At two elegant bridges, without e'er a river:
So, success to the humours of Donnybrook Fair!

*Alas, for faded glories. There's a Rugby-football ground
now where the fair was probably held. The present-day
semi-suburb has a television station and the new and
growing campus of University College, Dublin. Embassies
abound.*

*On the goings on at Donnybrook Fair the poet and
story-teller John Keegan, from the midland county of
Laois, cast a sombre eye:*

I was two days and a piece of one night at Donnybrook
Fair. I was told (and from previous descriptions I
believe it) that the fair this year was no more to the
carnivals of other days than the puppet Punch is to the
Colossus of Rhodes. Heaven knows it would be a
blessing if Donnybrook was sunk in hell, and expunged
forever from the map of our unfortunate country. I

had conceptions of vice, of profligacy and debauchery. I had read Eugène Sue and Lytton Bulwer and George Sand, but never did I dream of human debasement until I went to Donnybrook. In my opinion (and I try to be moderate) on last Thursday there were at least 40,000 females in Donnybrook: of these, I would be on my oath, there were at five o'clock in the evening 30,000 more or less intoxicated . . . You tell me of Irish virtue. I once gloried in the dreams of Irish modesty, but, alas, in Donnybrook my eyes were opened. I was grieved, I was humbled, I was mortified. Indeed, I will never again go to Donnybrook, or if I do, I never again will mingle in the vortex of degraded human beings which unfortunately contribute the great mass of the meeting. I saw hundreds of ladies and gentlemen there, but unless the depraved portion of this class (and there are *ladies* enough depraved in Dublin) they remained in their carriages and cars, and did not mingle at all amongst the mob. But people of the highest rank go to see the fair.

John Keegan, *Legends and Poems*, 1907

Donnybrook Fair

[6]

*That was sometime in the 1840s. But Keegan was a
gloomy man, a schoolmaster, and a misogynist who made
the mistake of marrying a woman whom he later described as a veritable Xantippe. And surely to St Laurence
O'Toole, the city's patron saint, there could not have been
that many frenzied females. Bacchantes?*

Three Poets on Dublin

*I group together three poets, and their varied tributes to
this city. First of all I listen to Donagh MacDonagh
whose father also was a poet. Thomas MacDonagh was
one of the signatories of the 1916 declaration of the Irish
republic and, for that reason, died before a British
firing-squad. Of P. H. Pearse and Thomas MacDonagh,
W. B. Yeats wrote:*

> This man had kept a school
> And rode our wingèd horse;
> The other his helper and friend
> Was coming into his force:
> He might have won fame in the end,
> So sensitive his nature seemed,
> So daring and sweet his thought.
>
> from 'Easter 1916'

*The fame he won was to be of another and more tragic
kind.*

*The father's memories and affections of place were of
the rich land of Tipperary: Norman country. The son
grew up in Dublin and, also, very much under the shadow
of the event that had ended his father's life. He could
talk most movingly, even disturbingly, of what it had felt
like to appear on public platforms as the orphaned son of
a patriot father.*

This poem makes clear his allegiance to and love for the Dublin streets:

DUBLIN MADE ME

Dublin made me and no little town
With the country closing in on its streets
The cattle walking proudly on its pavements
The jobbers, the gombeenmen and the cheats,

Devouring the fair-day between them
A public-house to half a hundred men
And the teacher, the solicitor and the bank-clerk
In the hotel bar drinking for ten.

Dublin made me, not the secret poteen still,
The raw and hungry hills of the West
The bare road flung over profitless bog
Where only a snipe could nest

Where the sea takes its tithe of every boat.
Bawneen and currach have no allegiance of mine,
Nor the cute, self-deceiving talkers of the South
Who look to the East for a sign.

The soft and dreary midlands with their tame canals
Wallow between sea and sea, remote from adventure,
And Northward a far and fortified province
Crouches under the lash of arid censure.

I disclaim all fertile meadows, all tilled land
The evil that grows from it and the good,
But the Dublin of old statutes, this arrogant city,
Stirs proudly and secretly in my blood.

§

An Ulsterman and the son of a bishop of the Church of Ireland, an Oxford classical scholar, a teacher in England, a producer with the BBC, Louis MacNeice when he

*thought of home may have thought of Carrickfergus in
County Antrim about which he wrote a fine poem. But
equally well he wrote of 'the laughter of the Galway sea/
Juggling with spars and bones irresponsibly'.*

*That last was in a poem called 'Train to Dublin', and
in another fine poem he defined to perfection the historic
character of the city, and, as he then saw it, its contemporary appearance:*

DUBLIN

> Grey brick upon brick,
> Declamatory bronze
> On sombre pedestals –
> O'Connell, Grattan, Moore –
> And the brewery tugs and the swans
> On the balustraded stream
> And the bare bones of a fanlight
> Over a hungry door
> And the air soft on the cheek
> And porter running from the taps
> With a head of yellow cream
> And Nelson on his pillar
> Watching his world collapse.
>
> This was never my town,
> I was not born nor bred
> Nor schooled here and she will not
> Have me alive or dead
> But yet she holds my mind
> With her seedy elegance,
> With her gentle veils of rain
> And all her ghosts that walk
> And all that hide behind
> Her Georgian façades –
> The catcalls and the pain,
> The glamour of her squalor,
> The bravado of her talk.

The lights jig in the river
With a concertina movement
And the sun comes up in the morning
Like barley-sugar on the water
And the mist on the Wicklow hills
Is close, as close
As the peasantry were to the landlord,
As the Irish to the Anglo-Irish,
As the killer is close one moment
To the man he kills,
Or as the moment itself
Is close to the next moment.

She is not an Irish town
And she is not English,
Historic with guns and vermin
And the cold renown
Of a fragment of Church Latin,
Or an oratorical phrase.
But O the days are soft,
Soft enough to forget
The lesson bitter learnt,
The bullet on the wet
Streets, the crooked deal,
The steel behind the laugh,
The Four Courts burnt.

Fort of the Dane,
Garrison of the Saxon,
Augustan capital
Of a Gaelic nation,
Appropriating all
The alien brought,
You give me time for thought
And by a juggler's trick

You poise the toppling hour –
O greyness run to flower,
Grey stone, grey water
And brick upon grey brick.

§

*Also from Ulster, from the County Monaghan, came the
poet Patrick Kavanagh, walking, as William Carleton
the novelist had done a century or so previously, to make
his own of the capital city.*

*For Kavanagh, Baggot Street constituted his village or
small town. At one end the Fairgreen: the splendid park
of St Stephen's Green. At the other end the bridge below
the town: the bridge over the Grand Canal. That street
he made particularly his own and it is quite possible that
his ghost may still walk there. Or so he is prepared to
tell us:*

If ever you go to Dublin town
In a hundred years or so
Inquire for me in Baggot Street
And what I was like to know.
O he was a queer one
Fol dol the di do,
He was a queer one
I tell you.

My great-grandmother knew him well,
He asked her to come and call
On him in his flat and she giggled at the thought
Of a young girl's lovely fall.
O he was dangerous
Fol dol the di do,
He was dangerous
I tell you.

On Pembroke Road look out for my ghost
Dishevelled with shoes untied,
Playing through the railings with little children
Whose children have long since died.
O he was a nice man
Fol dol the di do,
He was a nice man
I tell you.

Go into a pub and listen well
If my voice still echoes there,
Ask the men what their grandsires thought
And tell them to answer fair.
O he was eccentric
Fol dol the di do,
He was eccentric
I tell you.

He had the knack of making men feel
As small as they really were
Which meant as great as God had made them
But as males they disliked his air.
O he was a proud one
Fol dol the di do,
He was a proud one
I tell you.

If ever you go to Dublin town
In a hundred years or so
Sniff for my personality,
Is it vanity's vapour now?
O he was a vain one
Fol dol the di do,
He was a vain one
I tell you.

I saw his name with a hundred others
In a book in the library
He said he had never achieved
His potentiality.
O he was slothful
Fol dol the di do,
He was slothful
I tell you.

He knew that posterity has no use
For anything but the soul,
The lines that speak the passionate heart,
The spirit that lives alone.
O he was a lone one
Fol dol the di do,
Yet he lived happily
I tell you.

From Donnybrook to Ballsbridge by way of Herbert Park.
   Herbert Park, where Brendan Behan much loved to be on the grass and sun himself – is small, beautifully kept, never quite as crowded as St Stephen's Green which, being right at the centre of things, is one of the best-known showplaces or parading-grounds of the city.
   Dublin isn't badly off for parks and you can still walk safely in any of them. It has, of course, the Phoenix Park which we never tire of saying is the largest enclosed park in the world : and contains the zoo, the Peoples' Gardens, vast open spaces, and timber and deer and playing pitches, and the Wellington obelisk, and the residences of the Irish president and the US ambassador.
   To the great Duke of Ormonde as mentioned here by Maurice James Craig, the citizens, perhaps, should nod in gratitude for the Phoenix Park.

Ormonde's ideal . . . was an Ireland of Protestant
and (if possible) Catholic, whose greatest need was

peace, and the noblest outward sign of peace, public works. And as charity begins at home, so improvements were best placed where they would make the best showing in the capital itself. Any measure which would emphasise Dublin's position as the head and front of Ireland was in tune with the new policy. For it must be remembered that only now did Dublin become the capital in any modern sense. It was less than a century since Drogheda had been abandoned as a venue for Parliament . . . The Dublin Parliament of 1613, only fifty years before, was the first to be in any sense representative of the whole country; and it was also the first, by a natural consequence, in which any serious anti-English opposition was encountered. The ecclesiastical capital was, and still is, Armagh. For many a long year after 1660 there were whole tracts of the country which held little or no communication with Dublin.

But Ormonde's policy, half-consciously inspired by the Parisian example, was permanently successful in this sense: that Dublin became and remained an object of first interest for all important movements from now on. In the recent past, native Irish leaders such as Owen Roe O'Neill had conducted their strategy almost without reference to the capital as such. But even the Gaelic mind was now to learn the urban habit. Dublin, from being merely the chief garrison of the English Pale, was to become an object of pride and of contention to Irishmen of whatever race or creed.

As it stood in 1660, it was hardly an object of pride to anybody . . .

Maurice Craig, *Dublin 1660–1860 : A Social and Architectural History*, 1969

St Stephen's Green

The novelist George Moore was born in 1852, son of a notable landed family in the County Mayo. When in the novel A Drama in Muslin *(1886) he wrote of the plight of the daughters of the Anglo-Irish landed classes herded up like cattle to the husband-hunting at the Dublin Castle receptions he was thinking of the year 1882, when he was a man of thirty; and the eye that he cast on his own class and his own city was cold, very cold:*

The weary, the woebegone, the threadbare streets – yes, threadbare conveys the moral idea of Dublin in 1882. Stephen's Green, recently embellished by a wealthy nobleman with gravelled walks, mounds and ponds, looked like a school treat set out for the entertainment of charity children. And melancholy Merrion Square! broken pavements, unpainted halldoors, rusty area railings, meagre outside cars hidden almost out of sight in the deep gutters – how infinitely pitiful!

The Dublin streets stare the vacant and helpless stare of a beggar selling matches on a doorstep, and the feeble cries for amusement are like those of the child beneath the ragged shawl for the red gleam of a passing soldier's coat. On either side of you, there is a bawling ignorance or plaintive decay. Look at the houses! Like crones in borrowed bonnets some are fashionable with flowers in the rotting window frames – others languish in silly cheerfulness like women living on the proceeds of the pawnshop; others – those with brass plates on the doors – are evil-smelling as the prescriptions of the threadbare doctor, bald as the bill of costs of the servile attorney. And the souls of the Dubliners blend and harmonize with their connatural surroundings.

We are in a land of echoes and shadows. Lying, mincing, grimacing – careless of all but the pleasures of scandal and marriage, trailing their ignorance, arrogantly the poor shades go by. Gossip and waltz tunes are all that they know. Is there a girl or young man in Dublin who has read a play of Shakespeare, a novel of Balzac, a poem of Shelley? Is there one who could say for certain that Leonardo da Vinci was neither comic-singer nor patriot? – No. Like children, the young and the old run hither and thither, seeking in Tiddell oblivion of the Land League. Catholic in name, they curse the Pope for not helping them in their affliction; moralists by tradition, they accept at their parties women who parade their lovers to the town from the top of a tramcar. In Dublin there is baptism in tea and communion in a cutlet.

We are in a land of echoes and shadows. Smirking, pretending, grimacing, the poor shades go by, waving a mock-English banner over a waxwork show: policemen and bailiffs in front, landlords and agents behind, time-servers, Castle hirelings, panderers and worse on the box; nodding the while their dollish cardboard heads, and distributing to an angry populace, on either side, much bran and brogue. Shadows, echoes, and nothing more. See the girls! How their London fashions sit upon them; how they strive to strut and lisp like those they saw last year in Hyde Park. See the young men – the Castle bureaucrats – how they splutter their recollections of English plays, English scenes, English noblemen. See the pot-hatted Gigmen of the Kildare Street Club! The green flags of the League are passing; the cries of a new Ireland awake the dormant air; but the Gigmen foam at their windows and spit out mongrel curses on the land that refuses to call them Irishmen . . .

George Moore has brought us to the corner of Stephen's Green and Merrion Row and quite close to the Shelbourne Hotel, where so many of the debutantes or Muslin Martyrs, as he called them, once stayed during the Castle season. At this corner of the Green stands the very striking memorial by the sculptor Edward Delaney to Theobold Wolfe Tone, the father, it is frequently said, of the Irish Republic. The monument and its stone surround is sometimes known, in the easy way that Dubliners have, as Tonehenge.

Just about here, in 1916, the poet James Stephens watched some of the more enthusiastic of the disciples of Wolfe Tone in action.

I came to the barricade. As I reached it and stood by the Shelbourne hotel, which it faced, a loud cry came from the Park. The gates opened and three men ran out. Two of them held rifles with fixed bayonets. The third gripped a heavy revolver in his fist. They ran towards a motor car which had just turned the corner and halted it. The men with bayonets took position instantly on either side of the car. The man with the revolver saluted, and I heard him begging the occupants to pardon him, and directing them to dismount. A man and woman got down. They were again saluted and directed to go to the sidewalk. They did so . . .

I spoke to the man with the revolver. He was no more than a boy, not more certainly than twenty years of age, short in stature, with close curling red hair and blue eyes – a kindly-looking lad. The strap of his sombrero had torn loose on one side, and except while he held it in his teeth it flapped about his chin. His face was sunburnt and grimy with dust and sweat.

This young man did not appear to me to be acting from his reason. He was doing his work from a determination implanted previously, days, weeks perhaps, on his imagination. His mind was – where? It was not with his body. And continually his eyes were searching widely, looking for spaces, scanning hastily the clouds, the vistas of the streets, for something that did not hinder him, looking away for a moment from the immediacies and rigours which were impressed where his mind had been.

When I spoke he looked at me, and I know that for some seconds he did not see me. I said:

'What is the meaning of all this? What has happened?'

He replied collectedly enough in speech, but with that ramble and errancy clouding his eyes.

'We have taken the City. We are expecting an attack from the military at any moment, and those people', he indicated knots of men, women and children clustered towards the end of the Green, 'won't go home for me. We have the Post Office, and the Railways, and the Castle. We have all the City. We have everything.'

James Stephens, *The Insurrection in Dublin*, 1916

Custom House, from George's Quay

On the south side of the Green, from a window in the expansive stone front of number 86, it was said that Buck Whaley, an eighteenth-century layabout, leaped to land in the lap of a lady passing in a coach. The building has other, more respectable associations. Here is one of them:

— To return to the lamp, he said, the feeding of it is also a nice problem. You must choose the pure oil and you must be careful when you pour it in not to overflow it, not to pour in more than the funnel can hold.

— What funnel? asked Stephen.

— The funnel through which you pour oil into your lamp.

— That? said Stephen. Is that called a funnel? Is it not a tundish?

— What is a tundish?

— That. The . . . the funnel.

— Is that called a tundish in Ireland? asked the dean. I never heard the word in my life.

— It is called a tundish in Lower Drumcondra, said Stephen, laughing, where they speak the best English.

— A tundish, said the dean reflectively. That is a most interesting word. I must look that word up. Upon my word I must.

His courtesy of manner rang a little false, and Stephen looked at the English convert with the same eyes as the elder brother in the parable may have turned on the prodigal. A humble follower in the wake of clamorous conversions, a poor Englishman in Ireland, he seemed to have entered on the stage of Jesuit history when that strange play of intrigue and suffering and envy and struggle and indignity had been all but given through – a late-comer, a tardy spirit. From what had he set out? Perhaps he had been born and bred among serious dissenters, seeing salvation in

Jesus only and abhorring the vain pomps of the establishment. Had he felt the need of an implicit faith amid the welter of sectarianism and the jargon of its turbulent schisms, six principle men, peculiar people, seed and snake baptists, supralapsarian dogmatists? Had he found the true church all of a sudden in winding up to the end like a reel of cotton some fine-spun line of reasoning upon insufflation or the imposition of hands or the procession of the Holy Ghost? Or had Lord Christ touched him and bidden him follow like that disciple who had sat at the receipt of custom, as he sat by the door of some zinc-roofed chapel, yawning and telling over his church pence?

The dean repeated the word yet again.

— Tundish! Well now, that is interesting!

— The question you asked me a moment ago seems to me more interesting. What is that beauty which the artist struggles to express from lumps of earth, said Stephen coldly.

The little word seemed to have turned a rapier point of his sensitiveness against this courteous and vigilant foe. He felt with a smart of dejection that the man to whom he was speaking was a countryman of Ben Jonson. He thought:

— The language in which we are speaking is his before it is mine. How different are the words *home*, *Christ*, *ale*, *master*, on his lips and on mine! I cannot speak or write these words without unrest of spirit. His language, so familiar and so foreign, will always be for me an acquired speech. I have not made or accepted its words. My voice holds them at bay. My soul frets in the shadow of his language.

What James Joyce in A Portrait of the Artist as a Young Man *(1916) had the young Stephen Dedalus, rather nastily, thinking was that the Jesuit, Father*

Darlington, an Englishman and the model, it is said, for the dean in that novel, was a class of a poor man's John Henry Newman.

In the Fall of 1939, the present editor spent a while in Linden Convalescent Home near Blackrock by the sea in South Dublin city. Old-fashioned snobs still insist on placing it in County Dublin. On his last days in Linden at the time was the great Jesuit Father, Tom Finlay: apostle of agricultural co-operatives at the beginning of the century with Sir Horace Plunkett, George Russell (AE) the poet, and Patrick Gallagher of Dungloe – Paddy the Cope.

My memories of my conversations with the old priest I put into a short story called, oddly enough, 'A Room in Linden'. In this passage he is talking to the young man in the story about two of his Jesuit colleagues, or brothers in Christ:

— Darlington, he said, used to call on Hopkins to take him out for walks. Hopkins was forever and always complaining of headaches. What else can you expect, Darlington would say to him, immured up there in your room writing rubbish. I'm not so sure that Darlington wasn't right.

He is at that time just entering his Hopkins phase and if he wasn't afraid of that granite face, eyes sunken and black and burning, jawbones out rigid like a forked bush struck by lightning, he would defend the poet, quoting his sonnet about the windhover which, with some difficulty, he has just memorized. Yet it still is something to hear those names tossed about by a man who knew the men, and was a name himself . . . He searches for something neutral to say: Wasn't Hopkins always very scrupulous about marking students' papers?

— He was a neurotic Englishman, my good fellow.

They never could make up their minds between imperialism and humanitarianism. That's what has them the way they are. Darlington was English too, of course. The other sort. The complacent Englishman, thinking that only what is good can happen to him, and that all his works are good. Then a young upstart called Joyce put him in a book. That should have been a lesson to Darlington, if they have books in heaven or wherever he went to.

Joyce wrote of the cloistral, silver-veined prose of Newman; and here in that building from a window of which, it is alleged, Buck Whaley made that chivalrous, or merely amorous leap to the lady's lap, Newman presided for a while over the activities of a Catholic university. Round the corner in Harcourt Street the house in which he lived is now the headquarters of an advertising agency.

He was everything but happy here. Principally because of conflict with his employers, the Irish Catholic bishops who still own the great house, from which the gentleman jumped: no bishop has up-to-date equalled that caper. Newman wanted the best lecturers available. The bishops most certainly did not want any lecturer who smelled in the least of revolution: dreadful things had happened, to bishops and others, in France.

So that Newman's time here might have to some extent resembled what he would have called a scroll of lamentation. Yet he had great hopes for the Irish. Here in University Church, now notable for fashionable weddings, you can see his head in calm, cloistral marble. From that pulpit he may have spoken these words:

I look toward a land both old and young – old in its Christianity, young in its promise of the future: a nation which received grace before the Saxon came to Britain and which has never questioned it; a Church which comprehends in its history the rise and fall of

Canterbury and York, which Augustine and Paulinus found, and Pole and Fisher left behind them. I contemplate a people which has had a long night, and will have an inevitable day. I am turning my eye toward a hundred years to come, and I dimly see the Ireland I am gazing on become the road of passage and union between the two hemispheres, and the centre of the world. I see its inhabitants rival Belgium in populousness, France in vigour, and Spain in enthusiasm.

No man should ever, deliberately, make a prophecy. If one happens by accident and time proves it true, well and good. In the 1980s the ironic echoes of that passage are overpowering. But then G. K. Chesterton, who came over here in 1932 for the Eucharistic Congress in the Phoenix Park, afterwards wrote of Ireland as the last verdant outpost of Christianity. He called the book in which that appeared Christendom in Dublin. *On the same occasion John Count McCormack, in the Phoenix Park, sang* 'Panis Angelicus.'

§

Through 86 Stephen's Green, and through the Iveagh Gardens at the rear (another gift of the Guinness family to Dublin city, as is St Stephen's Green itself), a private way leads to what was once the main body of University College, Dublin. The campus has now moved south to Belfield, beyond Donnybrook and the Dodder river, and only a few remnants of the college remain here in Earlsfort Terrace. But the great oblong building had a lasting influence on many notable Irishmen of our time.

This was how Main Hall appeared to Brian O'Nolan, alias Flann O'Brien, alias Myles na Gopaleen (a man much given to Trinities), in his novel At Swim-Two-Birds *(1939):*

It was my custom to go into the Main Hall of the college and stand with my back to one of the steam-heating devices, my faded overcoat open and my cold hostile eyes flitting about the faces that passed before me. The younger students were much in evidence, formless and ugly in adolescence; others were older, bore themselves with assurance and wore clothing of good quality. Groups would form for the purpose of disputation and dissolve again quickly. There was much foot-shuffling, chatter and noise of a general or indeterminate character. Students emerging from the confinement of an hour's lecture would grope eagerly for their cigarettes or accept one with gratitude from a friend. Clerical students from Blackrock or Rathfarnham, black clothes and bowler hats, would file past civilly and leave the building by a door opening to the back where they were accustomed to leave the iron pedal-cycles. Young postulants or nuns would also pass, their eyes upon the floor and their fresh young faces dimmed in the twilight of their hoods, passing to a private cloakroom where they would spend the intervals between their lectures in meditation and pious practices. Occasionally there would be a burst of horseplay and a sharp cry from a student accidentally hurt. On wet days there would be an unpleasant odour of dampness, an aroma of overcoats dried by body-heat. There was a clock plainly visible but the hours were told by a liveried attendant who emerged from a small office in the wall and pealed a shrill bell similar to that utilized by auctioneers and street-criers; the bell served this purpose, that it notified professors – distant in the web of their fine thought – that their discourses should terminate . . .

The lighted rectangle of the doorway to the debate-hall was regarded by many persons not only as a receptacle for the foul and discordant speeches which they addressed to it, but also for many objects of a worthless nature – for example spent cigarette ends, old shoes, the hats of friends, parcels of damp horse dung, wads of soiled sacking and discarded articles of ladies' clothing not infrequently the worse for wear. Kelly on one occasion confined articles of his landlady's small-clothes in a neatly done parcel of brown paper and sent it through a friend to the visiting chairman, who opened it *coram populo* (in the presence of the assembly) and examined the articles fastidiously as if searching among them for an explanatory note, being unable to appraise their character instantaneously for two reasons, his failing sight and his status as a bachelor . . .

Since the Bloomsday of the Joyce centenary the head of James Joyce (by Marjorie Fitzgibbon), faces the place where the precise Stephen meditated on the English language; and there in St Stephen's Green joins the poet, James Clarence Mangan, whom Joyce so much admired, and the head (by Séamus Murphy of Cork) of Constance,

the Countess Markiewicz, who was part of the rebel garrison in 1916, just over there to the west in the College of Surgeons, and who with her sister, Eva Gore-Booth, was remembered by William Yeats in the long-ago light of evening in Lissadell. And joins also Thomas M. Kettle, college-friend of Joyce, who died in British uniform on the western front, and who wrote :

In wiser days, my darling rosebud, blown
To beauty proud, as was your mother's prime,
In that desired delayed incredible time,
You'll ask why I abandoned you, my own,
And dear heart that was your baby throne,
To dice with death. And Oh! they'll give you rhyme
And reason: some will call the thing sublime,
And some decry it in a knowing tone.

So here, while the mad guns curse overhead,
And tired men sigh, with mud for couch and floor,
Know that we fools, now with the foolish dead
Died not for flag, for King nor Emperor –
But for a dream, born in a herdsman's shed,
And for the secret scripture of the poor.

'To my Daughter, Betty: the Gift of God',
Poems and Parodies, 1916

Old Dublin

Geography can be imbibed in various ways and this old anonymous street-ballad takes you on a grand tour of the town, placing crafts and trades in the streets in which they had once concentrated. The pattern is, more or less, lost in the modern city, although it is still possible to be a banker in College Street or College Green, or to sell hosiery around High Street, if you are unperturbed by the Saturday crowds.

I am a roving sporting blade they call me Jack of All
    Trades,
I always placed my chief delight in courting pretty
    fair maids;
So when in Dublin I arrived to try for a situation,
I always heard them say it was the pride of all the
    nations.
I'm roving Jack of All Trades, of every trade of all
    trades,
And if you wish to know my name, they call me Jack
    of All Trades.

On George's Quay I first began and there became a
    porter.
Me and my master soon fell out which cut our
    acquaintance shorter.
In Sackville Street a pastry cook, in James's Street a
    baker.
In Cook Street I did coffins make, in Eustace Street a
    preacher.

In Baggot Street I drove a cab and there was well
    requited,
In Francis Street had lodging beds to entertain all
    strangers:
For Dublin is of high renown, or I am much
    mistaken.
In Kevin Street, I do declare, sold butter, eggs and
    bacon.

In Golden Lane I sold old shoes, in Meath Street was
    a grinder.
In Barrack Street I lost my wife, I'm glad I neer
    could find her.
In Mary's Lane I've dyed old clothes of which I've
    often boasted.
In that noted place, Exchequer Street, sold mutton
    ready roasted.

In Cole's Lane a jobbing butcher, in Dame Street
    was a tailor,
In Moore Street a chandler and on the Coombe a
    weaver,
In Church Street I did sell old ropes, on Redmond's
    Hill a draper,
In Mary Street sold 'bacco pipes, in Bishop Street, a
    Quaker.

In Peter Street I was a quack, in Greek Street was a
    grainer,
On the harbour I did carry sacks, in Werburgh Street,
    a glazier.
In Mud Island was a dairy boy, where I became a
    scooper,
In Capel Street a barber's clerk, in Abbey Street a
    cooper.

In Temple Bar I dressed old hats, in Thomas Street
    a sawyer,
In Pill Lane I sold the plate, in Green Street, an
    honest lawyer.
In Plunkett Street I sold cast clothes, in Bride's Alley
    a broker,
In Charles Street I had a shop, sold shovel, tongs
    and poker.

In College Street a banker was, and in Smithfield a
    drover,
In Britain Street a waiter and in George's Street a
    glover.
On Ormond Quay I sold old books, in King Street
    was a nailer,
In Townsend Street a carpenter, and in Ringsend a
    sailor.

In Liffey Street had furniture, with fleas and bugs I
    sold it,

And at the Bank a big placard I often stood to hold it.
In New Street I sold hay and straw and in Spitalfields
made bacon,
In Fishamble Street was busy at the trade of basket-
making.

In Summerhill a coachmaker, in Denzille Street a
gilder,
In Cork Street was a tanner, in Brunswick Street a
builder.
In High Street I sold hosiery, in Patrick Street sold all
blades.
So if you wish to know my name they call me Jack of
All Trades.

Flann O'Brien, *At Swim—Two—Birds*, 1939

William Carleton (1794–1869), author of Traits and
Stories of the Irish Peasantry, *came as a young man and
impoverished, and on foot, into Dublin city, and found his
first days and nights there somewhat lacking in creature
comforts. He was to become, as a young man called
W. B. Yeats wrote about the beginning of the century,
'The greatest novelist of Ireland by right of the most
Celtic eyes that ever gazed from under the brow of story-
teller.'*

*The young Carleton finds his way to a beggars' cellar
in the old city in the neighbourhood of Christchurch
Cathedral:*

When I got down to the cellar and looked about me I
was struck, but only for an instant, by the blazing fire
which glowed in the grate. My eyes then ran over the
scene about me . . . The inmates were mostly in bed,
both men and women, but still a good number of them
were up and indulging in liquors of every description,
from strong whiskey downwards. The beds were
mostly what are called shakedowns – that is, simple

straw, sometimes with a rag of sheet and sometimes with none. There were the lame, the blind, the dumb, and all who suffered from actual and natural infirmity; but in addition to these, there was every variety of impostor about me – most of them stripped of their mechanical accessories of deceit, but by no means all . . . Crutches, wooden legs, artificial cancers, scrofulous necks, artificial wens, sore legs . . . were hung up upon the walls of the cellar, and made me reflect upon the degree of perverted talent and ingenuity that must have been necessary to sustain such a mighty mass of imposture. Had the same amount of intellect, thought I, been devoted to the exercise of honest and virtuous industry, how much advantage in the shape of energy and example might not society have derived from it.

David J. O'Donoghue, *The Life of William Carleton*, 1896

The Ulster poet, Joseph Campbell (1879–1944), acquired another name from the title of one of his books, The Mountainy Singer, *poems mostly about the North with, perhaps, special reference to the Glens of Antrim. He came south to Dublin, lived for a while in London, came back to Dublin to become involved in revolutionary politics, spent years in bitter exile in New York, returned to live in Dublin to become devoted to, and to die in, the Dublin-Wicklow mountains in Glencree. From folklore, and from an older song, he took the Spanish lady, perhaps the King of Spain's daughter, from the shadowy arches of Galway to walk as a vision on the streets of Dublin.*

As I walked down through Dublin City
At the hour of twelve in the night,
Who should I spy but a Spanish lady,
Washing her feet by candlelight?
First she dipped them, and then she dried them,
Over a fire of ambery coal.

Never in all my life did I see
A maid so neat about the sole.

I stopped to peep, but the Watchman passed,
And says: Young fellow, the night is late.
Go home to bed, or I'll wrastle you
At a double trot through the Bridewell gate!
So I waved a kiss to the Spanish lady,
Hot as the fire of cramesy coal.
I've seen dark maids, though never one
So white and neat about the sole.

O, she's too rich for a Poddle swaddy,
With her tortoise comb and mantle fine.
A Hellfire buck would fit her better
Drinking brandy and claret wine.
I'm just a decent College sizar,
Poor as a sod of smouldery coal;
And how would I dress the Spanish lady
And she so neat about the sole.

O, she'd make a mott for the Provost Marshal,
Or a wife for the Mayor on his coach so high,
Or a queen of Andalusia,
Kicking her heel in the Cardinal's eye.
I'm blue as cockles, brown as herrings
Over a grid of glimmery coal,
And all because of the Spanish lady,
So mortial neat about the sole.

I wandered north, and I wandered south,
By Golden Lane and Patrick's Close,
The Coombe, Smithfield and Stoneybatter,
Back to Napper Tandy's house.
Old age has laid its hand upon me,
Cold as a fire of ashy coal –
And where is the lovely Spanish lady,
That maid so neat about the sole?

Austin Clarke (ed.), *The Poems of Joseph Campbell*, 1963

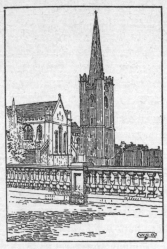

St. Patrick's Cathedral

Patrick Kennedy (1801–73), folklorist, story-teller and, in a way, novelist, came up from the Duffrey area of north-west Wexford to Dublin in the second decade of the nineteenth century to become a schoolteacher and, later, a bookseller and antiquarian. The Dublin he first saw was, mostly, the core of old Dublin from what is now O'Connell Bridge to the Phoenix Park, going south a little to embrace the great cathedrals of Christchurch and St Patrick :

I was disagreeably struck with the shabby, ruinous appearance of the streets in the Liberty; but was nearly terrified by the amazing height of St Patrick's steeple, after I had made my way to a clear view of it through the old rag and crockery fair held on the Coombe.

Then I added to my stock of knowledge by a glimpse of a soldier with an ordinary hat on his head, and cross belts over a blue coat standing sentry near the Deanery house. On inquiry I found he was only a policeman. I gazed with veneration on this old red building, owing to our great interest about its former occupant, Dean Swift . . .

I paid a visit to the outsides of St Patrick's, and Christ Church, and the Castle, and the College, and the old Parliament House, and the Royal Barracks to see the Highlanders on parade; and when the first impulses of curiosity were satisfied, and not a single known face to be seen, I began to feel the time dreadfully wearisome . . . This desolation fell on me at Carlisle Bridge; but looking up the river I bethought me of the Four Courts and the old book stalls. Oh, joy! I find there an odd volume of *Ossian* at one shilling, and, to enhance my good luck, Miss O'Reilly, who keeps a circulating library in the open air . . . offers to lend me *Waverly* at one penny per night . . .

Patrick Kennedy, *Evenings in the Duffrey*, 1869

Fresh from the place of his birth and youth on the remote Blasket Islands of that Irish-speaking corner of the south-west the young man comes to the city to join the Garda Síochána. Sixty or so years ago there were fewer people, the streets were cleaner and, to such a young fellow, a city bus, and even an automobile, might have been a bit of a wonder :

We reached O'Connell Bridge and got out. Trams and motors roaring and grating, newspaper-sellers at every corner shouting in the height of their heads, hundreds of people passing this way and that without stopping, and everyone of them, men and women, handsomely got up.

The trouble now was to cross the street. A man would make the attempt, then another, an eye up and an eye down, a step forward and a step back, until they would reach the other side.

'Oh Lord, George, this is worse than to be back

off the quay of the Blasket waiting for a calm moment to run in.'

He laughed. 'Here is a calm moment now,' he said suddenly. Off we went in a flutter, George gripping my arm; now forwards, now backwards, until we landed on the opposite side.

We walked on and I tell you my eyes opened wide when I saw above me every letter of the *Capitol* alight. 'Great God, George, look at the wonder above your head!' At that moment it went out, but again every letter was lit up till the whole *Capitol* was on fire. In deference to me, George let on he was as greatly astonished, like a mother petting her little child. Well, well, said I to myself, I must change and not show my wonder at anything else.

Maurice O'Sullivan, *Twenty Years A-Growing*
(trans. Moya Llewelyn Davies and George Thomson), 1933

The Liberties

To Adrian MacLoughlin we will give the privilege of leading us, in his invaluable Guide to Historic Dublin *(1979) – invaluable both for visitors and Dubliners and adopted Dubliners – into the most historic Liberties : the Earl of Meath's Liberties. Remembering Huguenot weavers and Dublin poplin and the like, he quotes Dean Swift writing on native industry :*

We'll rig in Meath Street, Egypt's haughty queen,
And Anthony shall court her in ratteen.

And goes on : Dublin's Liberties were areas of special privilege and special immunity from city jurisdiction in civil, but not criminal matters. Each had its own manor court, presided over by a 'seneschal'. The system originated under the Magna Carta, and the area concerned, whose geographical boundaries differed from time to time, was usually a spacious tract of land in the south-western part of the city. The Liberties included those of the Archbishop (St Sepulchre), Donore, Thomas Court (Earl of Meath), St Patrick's and Christ Church. The name 'St Sepulchre' had been given to the Archbishop's palace on the site of the present Kevin Street garda station. Donore was a place name, St Patrick's and Christ Church referred to the cathedrals, and Thomas Court is a reference to the monastery of St Thomas Beckett, whose lands were given to the Earl of Meath after the suppression of the institution, hence the alternative name. To add to the confusion caused by shifting boundaries and alternative names, there was a Liberty of Dublin, which included Donnybrook and stretched across the north side of the Liffey from Conyngham Road to East Wall. But the term is usually accepted as meaning only those privileged areas in the south-west, and of these the biggest was the Liberty of Donore, with 380 acres, including Mount Argus and Mount Jerome and parts of Crumlin; the smallest was that of Christ Church, with one and a half acres . . .

[Marsh's Library] was built in 1703 to the design of Sir William Robinson, and opened as a library in 1707. Its official name is the library of St Sepulchre, but the more common name commemorates Narcissus Marsh, Archbishop of Dublin, who founded and endowed it. He had resigned as provost of Trinity [College, Dublin] in 1683 because he found the high spirits of the students oppressive, and a distraction from his own studies.

The library contains about 25,000 printed books, including the personal library of Stillingfleet, bishop of Worcester, who died in 1699. There are also 200 manuscripts. The library stalls are still as they were

in the eighteenth century, giving the place an exceed-
ingly quaint air, with chained books and decorated
woodwork . . .

*Not only books and manuscripts does the old library in
the Liberties contain: but the ghost of the old scholar
and archbishop searching for a letter left for him, in a
book, by a young and, in his view, errant lady. The story
is repeated on the best authority, that of the present
librarian, Dr Muriel McCarthy in her book* All Graduates
and Gentlemen: Marsh's Library *(1980).*

The authority establishing the Library proclaimed:

'We order and appoint that all graduates and gentlemen
shall have free access to the said Library on the days
and hours before determined; provided they behave
themselves well . . .'

While Marsh was Archbishop of Dublin and living
as an old bachelor in the Palace of St Sepulchre he
arranged for his niece, young Grace Marsh, to look
after the housekeeping for him. Grace was only nine-
teen and probably found the Archbishop's life-style
and strict discipline rather depressing. On 10 Septem-
ber 1695, this rather sad entry appears in his diary:

> This evening betwixt 8 and 9 of the clock at night
> my niece Grace Marsh (not having the fear of God
> before her eyes) stole privately out of my house at
> St. Sepulchers and (as it is reported) was that night
> married to Chas Proby vicar of Castleknock in a
> tavern and was bedded there with him – Lord
> consider my affliction.

Grace lived to be eighty-five years old and it is nice
to know that she was, after her death, buried in the
same tomb with her uncle, the Archbishop. This
elopement has, of course, given rise to the ghost story:
that Grace regretted her elopement and left a letter for
Marsh in one of his books which he could not find.

His ghost still haunts the library searching through the books for Grace's letter. There is possibly one fascinating memento of Grace Marsh in the Library. Amongst Marsh's own books is a curious book entitled *Lachrimae lachrimarum or the Distillation of Teares shede for the Death of Prince Panaretus*. It was written by Joshua Sylvester and printed in London in 1613 . . . The work is a grim funeral elegy on the death of Prince Henry. The title-page is in black with the title shown in white, the head and tail of many pages have deep black borders with the sides illustrating skeletons and emblems of death. There is a signature on the endpapers: 'Grace Marsh Her Booke 1689'. It is quite possible that the Archbishop gave his young niece some improving literature and it might well have been one explanation for her subsequent elopement.

Through these old streets the market-women once cried their wares : and the weekend markets in Thomas Street and High Street, Francis Street, Meath Street and the Coombe can still be colourful. The cries of the dealers of the old days came to the attentive ears of a most remarkable man, who upset them (as Father Prout would have put it) into light verse :

APPLES

> Come buy my fine wares,
> Plums, apples and pears.
> A hundred a penny,
> In conscience too many:
> Come, will you have any?
> My children are seven,
> I wish them in Heaven:
> My husband's a sot,
> With his pipe and his pot,

Not a farthing will gain 'em,
And I must maintain 'em.

ONIONS

Come, follow me by the smell,
Here's delicate onions to sell;
I promise to use you well.
They make the blood warmer,
You'll feel like a farmer;
For this is every cook's opinion,
No savoury dish without an onion;
But lest your kissing should be spoiled,
Your onions must be thoroughly boiled:
   Or else you may spare
   Your mistress a share,
The secret will never be known:
   She cannot discover
   The breath of her lover,
But think it as sweet as her own.

HERRINGS

Be not sparing,
Leave off swearing.
Buy my herring
Fresh from Malahide,
Better never was tried.

Come, eat 'em with pure fresh butter and mustard,
Their bellies are soft, and as white as a custard.
Come, sixpence a dozen to get me some bread,
Or, like my own herrings, I soon shall be dead.

Jonathan Swift, *Verses made for Women who Cry
Apples, &c. (Works*, vol. viii, 1746)

*It is very much the lighter side of Jonathan Swift, Dean
of St Patrick's Cathedral, whose body rests, though
there is some slight doubt about that, in the cathedral,
as does the body of his beloved, or one of his beloveds,
Stella : Hester Johnson. The sombre Latin inscription
over Swift runs :*

Hic Depositum Est Corpus
Jonathan Swift, S.T.D.
Hujus Ecclesiae Cathedralis
Decani,
Ubi Saeva Indignatio
Ulterius Cor Lacerare Nequit.
Abi, Viator,
Et Imitare, Si Poteris
Strenuum Pro Virili
Libertatis Vindicatorem.

Roughly translated :

Here lies the body
of Jonathan Swift,
Dean of this Cathedral,
Where savage indignation

[39]

Can lacerate his heart no more.
Go, traveller,
And imitate, if you can,
His gallant fight for human liberty.

But the poet, Yeats, gave it a better turn:

Swift has sailed into his rest;
Savage indignation there
Cannot lacerate his breast.
Imitate him, if you dare,
World-besotted traveller; he
Served human liberty.

The Dissenters might not have agreed. Nor the ghost of the Archbishop and Primate, Narcissus Marsh, searching the Library for a letter left in a book, one among many.

Marsh died in 1713, and is buried in St Patrick's Cathedral, beside the Library he made and loved. Archbishop William King preached the funeral sermon:

Though a strict and rigid adherer to the service of our church, yet so far as I could observe, neither dissenters nor Roman Catholics did ever complain of him: on the contrary they looked on him as a mild and merciful adversary that rather chose to convert than hurt them. In his family he was an indulgent master, beloved of his servants, and ready to his power to do good offices not only to them, but to all men. The frequent addresses to him by petitions and other applications were so many, that one would wonder he had anything to spare for other occasions . . . These acts of charity were privately done, without noise or ostentation . . . such as the relieving fifty widows every first Friday of the month, together with many private pensions regularly paid the necessitous . . .

'But,' writes Archbishop Marsh's present-day librarian, Muriel McCarthy, in the work already mentioned,

one great Irishman, Jonathan Swift, did not share Archbishop King's charitable opinion of Narcissus Marsh. Swift blamed Marsh for his having to write the famous 'penitential letter' and for his lack of promotion in the Church of Ireland; he also held Marsh responsible for removing him from the management of the petition for the First Fruits of the Church of Ireland at the very moment when he had almost brought it to a successful conclusion. He never forgave Narcissus Marsh and wrote a spiteful, 'Character of Primate Marsh' about three years before Marsh's death.

Swift wrote: 'Marsh has the reputation of most profound and universal learning; this is the general opinion, neither can it be easily disproved. An old rusty iron-chest in a banker's shop, strongly lockt and wonderful heavy, is full of gold; this is the general opinion, neither can it be disproved, provided the key be lost, and what is in it be wedged so close that it will not by any motion discover the metal by the clinking. Doing good is his pleasure; and as no man consults another in his pleasures, neither does he in this . . . without all passions but fear, to which of all others he hath least temptation, having nothing to get or to lose; no posterity, relation or friend to be solicitous about; and placed by his station above the reach of fortune or envy . . . He is the first of human race, that with great advantages of learning, piety and station ever escaped being a great man . . . He is so wise to value his own health more than other men's noses, so that the most honourable place at his table is much the worst, especially in summer . . . No man will be either glad or sorry at his death, except his successor.'

Muriel McCarthy, All Graduates and Gentlemen: Marsh's Library, 1980

*And Swift expires, Johnson wrote, a gibberer and a show;
and now we know that his ailment was curable had the
doctors then but known; and he went, as he had
prophesied, like the decaying elms, he withered at the top.
Not so far away is the famous St Patrick's psychiatric
hospital, sometimes known as Swift's hospital because a
bequest of his financed its foundation.*

*There are many ghosts in these old streets, and it makes
for more happiness to think of the great Dean as Pope,
in imitation of Martial, amusingly imagined him, living
the happy life of a country parson:*

> Parson, these things in thy possessing
> Are better than a bishop's blessing.
> A wife that makes conserves; a steed
> That carries double where there's need:
> October store, and best Virginia,
> Tithe pig, and mortuary guinea:
> Gazettes sent gratis down, and frank'd,
> For which thy patron's weekly thank'd:
> A large concordance (bound long since),
> Sermons to Charles the First, when prince;
> A chronicle of ancient standing;
> A Chrysostom to smooth thy band in;
> The polyglot – three parts – my text,
> Howbeit – likewise – now to my next,
> Lo here the Septuagint – and Paul,
> To sum the whole – the close of all.
> He that has these may pass his life,
> Drink with the squire, and kiss his wife;
> On Sundays preach, and eat his fill;
> And fast on Fridays, if he will;
> Toast church and queen, explain the news
> Talk with Church-wardens about pews,
> Pray heartily for some new gift,
> And shake his head at Doctor Swift.

In the 1940s and 1950s the literati of Dublin used to congregate, under the ferrule of the great R. M. Smyllie, in the Palace Bar and later in the Pearl Bar in Fleet Street, Dublin, of course. R.M. was then editor of the Irish Times, *and great in every sense of the word.*

A sort of parlour or pub game went on for a while in the Palace and the Pearl: the composition of a poem about a character who was considered to be passing forever from the Dublin scene: like the Last of the Gleemen that Yeats wrote about but not, perhaps, as respectable. She was the Last of the Old-fashioned Hures: anglicé, whores. Every gentleman, or whatever, composed a verse and it was M. J. MacManus, scholar, bibliophile, literary editor, who was responsible for:

> The Dean of St Patrick's Cathedral
> Flung open his old-fashioned dures,
> And the ghost of Dean Swift
> Toddled forth in his shift
> To the last of the old-fashioned hures.

Ghosts, ghosts, ghosts!

As for the Palace Bar in the Forties and the Pearl Bar (now extinct) in the Fifties: you went there if you wanted to find out what Irish literature was currently about. You could also have read books, but going to the pubs was easier and much more fun. Yeats, who was no frequenter of pubs, was quite ludicrously nasty about the central figure of the group in the Palace:

> Some have known a likely lad
> That had a sound fly-fisher's wrist
> Turn to a drunken journalist . . .

That was a most outrageous thing to say about R. M. Smyllie who was, in our times, one of the great editors in these islands, and who gathered round him, in newspaper office and adjacent tavern, an interesting group of writers, artists, painters, journalists, and common-or-garden Dublin wits, to name just some of whom is to evoke an era in the history of literary Dublin: M. J. MacManus, Brinsley MacNamara, Sean O'Sullivan, Flann O'Brien, and Patrick MacDonagh, Donagh MacDonagh, Seamus O'Sullivan . . . et alii aliorum.

Tom Corkery is the pseudonym of the man who manages the cinema contained in the exquisite eighteenth-century building, the Rotunda, which gave its name, without prejudice, to the famous lying-in hospital, situate where O'Connell Street and Parnell Street meet; and where Charles Stewart Parnell stands, at the foot of his oddly shaped pillar, supervising the onward march of a nation to which, he said, no man had the right to set a boundary.

It is a hoary half-joke that his uplifted hand points straight to the door of a public house.

As his book, Tom Corkery's Dublin *demonstrates, the masked manager escapes now and again from the*

*movies to roam the streets like the oriental caliph; and to
cast on Dublin a warm and attentive eye.*

His happiest days may have been in the Fifties:

As you walked the Dublin streets of the Fifties you
became aware of a fairly amiable (most times) con-
glomeration of separate quarters, each with a certain
faintly defined but sure hierarchical order of its own.
Everybody seemed fairly easily ensconced in his own
scene, unenvying of his neighbour. Yet the poet could
and did share the same pub with the peasant, and no
man had need of looking up, down or askance at his
fellow man . . . Patrick Kavanagh could be heard dis-
coursing in MacDaid's of Harry Street on such esoteric
subjects as professional boxing, the beauty of Ginger
Rogers, or the dire state of Gaelic football in Ulster.
Flann O'Brien could be heard in Neary's or the Scotch
House on any subject known to man . . . Brendan
Behan could be heard everywhere. God could be heard
in his heaven, and adolescent people, except on
Christmas Eve and New Year's Eve, could only be
heard where they were meant to be heard, in Croke
Park, or Dalymount, or the goings-on in the local hall.

And this is how Tom Corkery sees his mother, Dublin:

Dublin is not, thank Heaven, a queen among cities·
Rather is she a garrulous pleasure-loving provincial
lady of good family, settling comfortably into middle-
age, putting on too much weight in the wrong places.
There is enough malice in her to keep her conversation
interesting, and hospitality is for her more a pleasure
than a duty. Like all provincial ladies she loves the fuss
of visitors; she will flatter them to their faces, gossip
about them behind their backs, and is as much flattered
as annoyed if, when they leave, they make snide

remarks about her. The only unforgivable thing is to say nothing at all about her.

An old bag of words, but mother and foster-mother of some famous sons and with no intention of letting you forget the fact. She will never tire of showing you where her James used to walk, recalling what her Seán used to say, how her Willie and George and Oscar used to behave; she will breathe her George Bernard down your ear until you scream for mercy. And she will blandly forget that when she had them she used to clip their ears every time they opened their mouths. But you cannot help liking the loquacious old dame, with her long-winded reminiscences and her senti-mental keepsakes all over the drawing-room. Whatever her failings parsimony is not one of them; dinner or no dinner, she dines at seven.

Her mornings are still elegant, not too harsh, not too obtrusive. There is not too much rattle, not too much clangour; a gentle susurration, the gently-refined invitation to be up and about. If sirens call they do so in muted half-hearted fashion, as though they are apprehensive of being prosecuted for disturbing the peace, and church bells interpolate occasional reminders that not by bread alone doth man live. People stop and talk to each other, maybe not too worried whether they get to their work on time. Indeed, one suspects, quite a few do not make it at all.

Not to worry. It is the real motto of the town, the explanation of its haphazard growth, and of its survival through a thousand years of very worrying history. For Dublin's was not a natural birth; the Danes who established it did so, not as the capital of Ireland but rather as a defence against Ireland. Nor did it have a natural growth, as normal towns grow . . .

Tom Corkery's Dublin, 1980

The Coombe and the Liffey

The famous comedian, Jimmy O'Dea, and his friend and colleague, Harry O'Donovan, brought back out of the shadows, and gave a new life to, the legendary lady and street-trader, Biddy Mulligan, the Pride of the Coombe. An old song was refurbished, and on the stage in the old Olympia, and on gramophone records, Mrs Mulligan went here and there, appeared in court, talked to fellow-Dubliners and rural types (culchies), even ventured into the fastnesses of the North to encounter her imitator, Mrs Maxwell from sweet Sandy Row, the creation, admittedly in parody, of Richard Hayward, the Ulster singer and author of excellent travel books:

I'm a thumping fine widow, I live in a spot,
In Dublin they call it the Coombe.
My shops and my stalls are laid out on the street,
And my palace consists of one room . . .

At Patrick Street corner, for forty-six years,
I've stood there, I'm telling no lie:
And while I was there, nobody would dare
To say green was the white of me eye . . .

You may travel from Clare to the County Kildare,
From Drogheda down to Macroom.
But where will you see a fine widow like me,
Biddy Mulligan, the Pride of the Coombe . . .

And I have a son, John, a great hand with the fife,
He belongs to the Longford Street Band.
It would do your heart good for to see him march out
When the band goes to Dollymount Strand . . .

Anon.

[47]

If John Mulligan had made that journey by helicopter (a vast unlikelihood!) he could have surveyed a most interesting section of the city: from the oldest of the old streets to the Bull Island and the edge of the salt sea, and the vision of Howth Head lying there across the narrow water. Edmund Spenser landed somewhere over there when he came to Ireland on a visit that was to be rewarding and fruitful and, ultimately, tragic. Granuaile, Grace O'Malley, the Connacht sea-queen of the time of Elizabeth I, called there at the great castle and was not made welcome: and the residents of the Castle were to commemorate for a long time that error in etiquette.

In the early years of the century a young man went walking on the Bull Island:

He was alone. He was unheeded, happy and near to the wild heart of life. He was alone and young and wilful and wildhearted, alone amid a waste of wild air and brackish waters and the seaharvest of shells and tangle and veiled grey sunlight and gayclad lightclad figures of children and girls and voices childish and girlish in the air.

A girl stood before him in midstream, alone and still, gazing out to sea. She seemed like one whom magic had changed into the likeness of a strange and beautiful seabird. Her long slender bare legs were delicate as a crane's and pure save where an emerald trail of seaweed had fastened itself as a sign upon the flesh. Her thighs, fuller and softhued as ivory, were bared almost to the hips where the white fringes of her drawers were like featherings of soft white down. Her slateblue skirts were kilted boldly about her waist and dovetailed behind her. Her bosom was as a bird's soft and slight, slight and soft as the breast of some darkplumaged dove. But her long fair hair was girlish: and girlish and touched with the wonder of mortal beauty, her face.

She was alone and still, gazing out to sea: and when she felt his presence and the worship of his eyes her eyes turned to him in quiet sufferance of his gaze, without shame or wantonness. Long, long she suffered his gaze and then quietly withdrew her eyes from his and bent them towards the stream, gently stirring the water with her foot hither and thither. The first faint noise of gently moving water broke the silence, low and faint and whispering, faint as the bells of sleep; hither and thither: and a faint flame trembled on her cheek.

— Heavenly God! cried Stephen's soul in an outburst of profane joy.

That was, once again, Stephen Dedalus in James Joyce's A Portrait of the Artist as a Young Man.

But John Mulligan's hypothetical helicopter is still over the Liffey and the Liberties. From it we may view some of the action down by the Liffeyside in the eighteenth century:

Among the lower orders, a feud and deadly hostility had grown up between the Liberty boys or tailors and weavers of the Coombe, and the Ormond boys or butchers who lived in Ormond market, on Ormond quay, which caused frequent conflicts; and it is in the memory of many now living that the streets, and particularly the quays and bridges, were impassable in consequence of the battles of these parties. The weavers, descending from the upper regions beyond Thomas Street, poured down on their opponents below; they were opposed by the butchers, and a contest commenced on the quays which extended from Essex to Island bridge. The shops were closed; all business suspended; the sober and peaceable compelled to keep their houses; and those whose occasions led them through the streets where the belligerents were engaged were stopped, while the war of stones and other missiles was carried on across the river, and the bridges were taken and retaken by the hostile parties. It will hardly be believed that for whole days the intercourse of the city was interrupted by the feuds of these factions. The few miserable watchmen, inefficient for any purpose of protection, looked on in terror, and thought themselves well acquitted of their duty if they escaped from stick and stone . . .

At one time, the Ormond boys drove those of the Liberty up to Thomas Street, where, rallying, they repulsed their assailants, and drove them back as far as the Broadstone, while the bridges and quays were strewed with the maimed and wounded. On May 11, 1790, one of those frightful riots raged for an entire Saturday on Ormond quay, the contending parties struggling for the mastery of the bridge; and nightfall having separated them before the victory was decided, the battle was renewed on the Monday following . . .

While it is heartening to know that the butchers and weavers observed the Sabbath, it is gruesome to read on in John Edward Walsh's Ireland Sixty Years Ago (1847), to find out that kneecapping is not just an elegancy of our happy time :

These feuds terminated sometimes in frightful excesses. The butchers used their knives not to stab their opponents, but for the purpose then common in the barbarous state of Irish society, to hough or cut the tendon of the leg, thereby rendering the person incurably lame for life. On one occasion, after a defeat of the Ormond boys, those of the Liberty retaliated in a manner still more barbarous and revolting. They dragged the persons they seized to their market, and, dislodging the meat they found there, hooked the men by the jaws, and retired, leaving the butchers hanging on their own stalls.

The eighteenth-century procession that brought Larry to dance the last minuet, possibly where Stephen's Green now is, would have passed from Kilmainham Jail through the heart of the old city and swung to the right at the statue of King William, Prince of Orange, in College Green. The statue is no longer there : the victim, like the Nelson pillar, and the Gough equestrian statue in the Park, of the patriotic involvement in urban renewal. On that occasion Dublin Opinion *said that King William left Dublin by air early this morning.*

The night before Larry was stretched,
The boys they all paid him a visit;
A bit in their sacks, too, they fetched,
They sweated their duds till they riz it;
For Larry was always the lad,
When a friend was condemned to the squeezer,
But he'd pawn all the togs that he had

Just to help the poor boy to a sneezer,
And moisten his gob 'fore he died.

"Pon my conscience, dear Larry,' says I,
'I'm sorry to see you in trouble,
And your life's cheerful noggin run dry
And yourself going off like its bubble.'
'For the neckcloth I don't care a button,
And by this time tomorrow you'll see
Your Larry will be dead as mutton:
All for what? 'Kase his courage was good.'

The boys they came crowding in fast;
They drew their stools close round about him.
Six glims round his coffin they placed,
He couldn't be well waked without 'em.
I asked if he was fit to die
Without having duly repented:
Says Larry: 'That's all in my eye
And all by the clergy invented
To make a fat bit for themselves.'

Then the cards being called for, they played
Till Larry found one of them cheated;
Quick he made a hard rap at his head,
The lad being easily heated:
'So ye chates me bekase I'm in grief!
O! Is that, by the Holy, the rason?
Soon I'll give you to know, you damned thief,
That you're cracking your jokes out of sason,
And scuttle your nob with my fist.'

Then in came the priest with his book,
He spoke him so smooth and so civil.
Larry tipped him a Kilmainham look
And pitched his big wig to the divil.
Then raising a little his head
To get a sweet drop of the bottle,

And, pitiful sighing, he said:
'O! the hemp will be soon round my throttle
And choke my poor windpipe to death.'

So mournful these last words he spoke
We all vented our tears in a shower.
For my part I thought my heart broke
To see him cut down like a flower.
On his travels we watched him next day,
O! the hangman I thought I could kill him.
Not one word did our poor Larry say,
Nor changed till he came to King William,
Och! my dear, then his colour turned white.

When he came to the nubbling chit,
He was tucked up so neat and so pretty,
The rumbler jugged off from his feet
And he died with his face to the city.
He kicked too, but that was all pride,
For soon you might see 'twas all over:
And, as soon as the noose was untied,
Then at darkey we waked him in clover
And sent him to take a ground sweat.

                                        Anon.

Francis Sylvester Mahony, neither Dubliner nor Dublin-man but a Corkman or Corkonian, translated (or, as he would have said, upset) that classical Dublin elegy into French under the title 'La Mort de Socrate'.

Mahony invented the character of Father Prout, parish priest of Watergrasshill, North Cork, and became himself known as Father Prout. Of Larry, the Dublinman, in his role of Socrates he had somewhat to say:

Ireland has produced a specimen of consummate proficiency in the grand fundamental maxims of utilitarianism and philosophy, exemplified in the calm composure, dignified tranquillity, and instructive self-possession with which death may be encountered after a life of usefulness. For the benefit and comfort of our allies, the French, I have taken some pains to initiate them, through the medium of a translation, into the workings of an Irish mind unfettered by conscientious scruples on the threshold of eternity.

The Works of Father Prout (the Revd Francis Mahony), 1836

Mahony's friend, the eminent Mr W. M. Thackeray, cast a kindly eye on Dublin and on all Ireland in his ever-delightful Irish Sketch Book. *He was an easygoing traveller and would sooner read a newspaper or a chap-book than climb a hill or seek the source of a river : and here he is enjoying a quiet Dublin morning in the early 1840s:*

This then is the chief city of the aliens. The hotel to which I had been directed is a respectable old edifice, much frequented by families from the country, and where the solitary traveller may likewise find society. For he may either use the Shelbourne as an hotel or a boarding-house, in which latter case he is comfortably accommodated at the very moderate daily charge of six and eightpence. For this charge a copious breakfast is provided for him in the Coffee-room, a perpetual luncheon is likewise there spread, a plentiful dinner is ready at six o'clock; after which, there is a drawing-room and a rubber of whist, with *tay* and coffee and cakes in plenty to satisfy the largest appetite. The hotel is majestically conducted by clerks and other officers; the landlord himself does not appear after the honest comfortable English fashion, but lives in a private mansion hard by, where his name may be read inscribed on a brass-plate, like that of any other private gentleman.

A woman melodiously crying, Dublin Bay Herrings,

passed just as we came to the door, and as that fish is famous throughout Europe I seized the earliest opportunity and ordered a broiled one for breakfast. It merits all its reputation: and in this respect I should think the Bay of Dublin is far superior to its rival of Naples – are there any herrings in Naples Bay? Dolphins there may be, and Mount Vesuvius to be sure is bigger than even the Hill of Howth, but a dolphin is better in a sonnet than at a breakfast, and what poet is there that, at certain periods of the day, would hesitate in his choice between the two.

§

The Brewery: the world knows the Brewery and the sanative merits of its black, cream-topped product; although many a man will argue that Dublin (and the world) have never been the same since the river-barges that carried the wooden kegs from the Brewery to the docks were replaced by motor-trucks: the wooden kegs in time, and as part of the continuing process of degeneration and decay, to be replaced by metal containers. At the period of the momentous change from barges to trucks, the great humorous magazine Dublin Opinion, *child of the minds of Charlie Kelly (C.E.K.) and Tom Collins, printed a drawing showing a well-dressed gentleman standing on the last of the barges as it went down the Liffey towards the sea. The caption read:*

And slowly answered Arthur from the barge:
The old order changeth, yielding place to new.

And the Arthur was not the man from Cadbury Hill but the even perhaps more immortal Arthur Guinness.

[55]

Dublin Opinion *was part of the life of the city from the early Twenties for forty or so years. It is now, alas, no more, nor are those two talented, humorous lovable men.*

For the great hymn of praise for the product of the Brewery we go again to Flann O'Brien alias Myles na Gopaleen alias Brian O'Nolan in At Swim-Two-Birds. *Three Dublin* segocias *(Lat. Socius), Furriskey, Shanahan, and Lamont are discussing poetry :*

'The name or title of the pome I am about to recite, gentlemen', said Shanahan with leisure priest-like in character, 'is a pome by the name of the "Workman's Friend". By God you can't beat it. I've heard it praised by the highest. It's a pome about a thing that's known to all of us. It's about a drink of porter . . .'

He arose holding out his hand and bending his knee beneath him on the chair.

> 'When things go wrong and will not come right,
> Though you do the best you can,
> When life looks black as the hour of night –
> A PINT OF PLAIN IS YOUR ONLY MAN.'

'By God, there's a lilt in that,' said Lamont.

'Very good indeed,' said Furriskey. 'Very nice.'

'I'm telling you it's the business,' said Shanahan. 'Listen now.'

> 'When money's tight and it's hard to get
> And your horse has also ran,
> When all you have is a heap of debt –
> A PINT OF PLAIN IS YOUR ONLY MAN.
>
> When health is bad and your heart feels strange,
> And your face is pale and wan,
> When doctors say that you need a change,
> A PINT OF PLAIN IS YOUR ONLY MAN.'

'There are things in that poem that make for what you call *permanence*. Do you know what I mean, Mr Furriskey?'

'There's no doubt about it, it's a grand thing,' said Furriskey. 'Come on, Mr Shanahan, give us another verse. Don't tell me that is the end of it.'

'Can't you listen,' said Shanahan.

> 'When food is scarce and your larder bare
> And no rashers grease your pan,
> When hunger grows as your meals are rare –
> A PINT OF PLAIN IS YOUR ONLY MAN.'

'What do you think of that now?'

'It's a pome that'll live,' called Lamont, 'a pome that'll be heard and clapped when plenty more . . .'

'But wait till you hear the last verse, man, the last polish-off,' said Shanahan. He frowned and waved his hand . . .

'In time of trouble and lousy strife
You have still got a darlint plan,
You still can turn to a brighter life –
A PINT OF PLAIN IS YOUR ONLY MAN!

'Did you ever hear anything like it in your life,' said Furriskey. 'A pint of plain, by God, what! Oh, I'm telling you, Casey was a man in twenty thousand, there's no doubt about that. He knew what he was at, too true he did. If he knew nothing else, he knew how to write a pome. A pint of plain is your only man.'

'Didn't I tell you he was good?' said Shanahan. 'Oh by Gorrah you can't cod me.'

'There's one thing in that poem, *permanence*, if you know what I mean. That pome, I mean to say, is a poem that'll be heard wherever the Irish race is wont to gather . . .'

Literary Dublin

Sometime in the Fifties a change took place in the literary landscape of Dublin. The sour isolationism of neutrality, an isolationism so favourable to the censoring mind, was gone and the country was beginning to take its place – and peace to Robert Emmet and his epitaph – among the nations of the earth. The younger poets, say Thomas Kinsella and John Montague (Séamus Heaney had not yet come South), displayed a desire to walk at some distance from the dominating shadow of the Tower of Ballylee. In a wonderful burst of productivity Austin Clarke was to spread his ageing eagle's wings and, by a series of superb satirical poems to startle the young fellows into realizing that this was no mere medievalist, however skilful and cunning, lost forever on the Rock of

Cashel, but a witty, modern, urbane poet. For instance,
this portrait of a lady dying in age and poverty having,
through her lifetime, liberally donated her money to the
welfare of the foreign missions, is very far away from any
form of Celtic romanticism :

MISS MARNELL

No bells rang in her house. The silver plate
Was gone. She scarcely had a candle-wick,
Though old, to pray by, ne'er a maid to wait
At all. She had become a Catholic
So long ago, we smiled, did good by stealth,
Bade her good day, invited her to tea
With deep respect. Forgetting her loss of wealth,
She took barmbrack and cake so hungrily,
We pitied her, wondered about her past.
But her poor mind had not been organized;
She was taken away, fingering to the last
Her ivory decades. Every room surprised:
Wardrobes of bombazine, silk dresses, stank:
Cobwebby shrouds, pantries, cupboard, bone-bare.
Yet she had prospering money in the bank,
Admiring correspondents everywhere,
In Ireland, Wales, the Far East, India;
Her withered hand was busy doing good
Against our older missions in Africa.
False teeth got little acid from her food:
But scribble helped to keep much mortar wet
For convent, college, higher institution,
To build new churches or reduce their debt.
The figure on her cross-cheque made restitution
For many sins. Piled on her escritoire
Were necessary improvements, paint-pot, ladder
And new coats for Maynooth, in a world at war,
Circulars, leaflets, pleas that made her madder

To comfort those who need for holy living
Their daily post: litterings, flyblown, miced
In corners, faded notes of thanksgiving,
All signed – 'Yours gratefully, in Jesus Christ.'

from *Too Great a Vine*, 1957

In 1957 Clarke was writing in the magazine Irish
Writing, *then under the editorship of Sean J. White:*

When I was in my early twenties I visited Paris for the
first time and met Stephen Dedalus there. I remember
well the evening on which he told me dolefully that
of all the thoroughfares of our native city he preferred
Capel Street . . .

Only recently have I found that Capel Street meant
much to me when I still went bare-kneed. All the way
from Drumcondra, through Upper and Lower Dorset
Street and Bolton Street, that thoroughfare kept
changing its name, becoming Capel Street as far as
Grattan Bridge, renaming itself Parliament Street for
a short distance and ending not ingloriously at the City
Hall. Along the left-hand side of Capel Street, which
had several sweet-shops, my sister Eileen and I walked
slowly during a few weeks for I had hired her as my
story-teller before I could read very well. The rate was
sixpence for twenty fairy-tales, but I must have been
able to count because I insisted on getting full value
for my money and the transaction was never
repeated . . .

*Right into our own time (almost), Austin Clarke, who
had a sort of medieval and humorous anti-clericalism,
favoured the great black hat that was once, in London
and Dublin, the sign of the artist and intellectual. W. B.
Yeats did so, in his time, having picked up the style from
the poets with whom he learned his trade, companions of
the Cheshire Cheese. Clarke also favoured a dark, rather*

clerical sort of overcoat. Which led to cases of mistaken identity. Which delighted him :

I am used to being mistaken for a clergyman and so I am no longer embarrassed by the respect paid to my cloth. As a Dublin youth, ignorant of new London literary ways, I believed that a poet must wear a wide-brimmed black hat and grave suit. Sometimes as I cycled along country roads, I was saluted by carter or stonebreaker, so I consulted a clerical student who was an intimate friend of mine. He told me what to do in order to spare the feelings of any passers-by who might salute me. For a year or so after this ordination, a young priest always raises his hat; gradually he learns only to touch it; then he moves his hand only as far as his shoulder – and at last a mere showing of his right palm suffices . . . Frequently, as I walk along the city streets, I am saluted, and in the suburbs, motorists, lorry-drivers, cyclists and small boys pay me undue respect. Clergymen on their auto-cycles give me a professional nod, or glance at me quickly, as they come out of city cinemas in the afternoon. Sometimes I am tempted to take vicarious advantage of my old-fashioned poetic garb. When I draw my black muffler close to hide my lack of celluloid collar, I am offered a seat immediately in an over-crowded bus, receive attention in tea-shops, quicker small sherries in the larger hotels – and I need never wait more than a few seconds outside a telephone booth.

Also sheltering under the aesthetic black hat, Robert Farren (Roibeárd Ó Faracháin) walks the streets of his native city and thinks that 'a dream may be sweet in Wicklow Street as a dream in a Wicklow valley : and the sworded Seraphim ring Rathgar, and Christ's eyes blind yours in Bull Alley.'

*And thinks when he looks down from a high window
on the people moving in the street, of the flowers in the
splendid Peoples' Gardens in the Phoenix Park:*

> If the flowers in the Peoples' Gardens
> should hoist their green stalks up
> and walk along the pathways,
> dahlia, pink, kingcup,
>
> they could not bring more colour
> than the colours of the peoples' heads,
> the silk-ladder blacks, the nut-browns,
> the yellows, the glinting reds,
>
> which burn between me and the sun there
> like borders of seagulls' wings,
> with the blond heads, double-lustred
> like pearls in platinum rings.
>
> They could not bring more dancing
> than the gleaming, dancing heads
> the silk-ladder blacks, the glancing
> yellows and the glinting reds.
>
> Colours of the heads on the pathways
> under September's sun
> are the City's Dancing Gardens
> Out-gardening Babylon.

from Roibeárd Ó Faracháin,
Rime, Gentlemen, Please, 1945

*In his last years Frank O'Connor (a Corkman) was a quiet
but splendid part of the Dublin scene, clad in fine tweeds,
clutching a stout stick and striding like a king along the
banks of the Grand Canal between the bridges of Leeson
Street and Baggot Street.*

When I ask myself what are the things which endear
me to this particular portion of the world where I
spend my days, I find them pitiably few. I write this

in a room which looks towards Dunleary (Dún Laoghaire or Kingstown) across the wide reaches of Merrion Strand, and I remember that this is the strand where in the eighth-century saga of *Da Derga's Hostel* the British outlaws landed, and that if I walk out a mile or two the Sandymount houses will slip out of sight and the mountains will rise up with those foothills where the hostel is supposed to have stood, on the Dodder bank, and its firelight shone through the spokes of the chariot wheels outside it. I remember that Stephen Dedalus in *Ulysses* walked here, as did Mr Bloom; that an English lad called L. A. G. Strong spent his holidays in Kingstown (Dún Laoghaire or Dunleary) and recorded them later in a few perfect short stories like *Prongs* and *The English Captain*, and that on Dalkey Hill above it another boy called George Bernard Shaw suddenly asked himself why he went on saying his prayers.

Frank O'Connor, *Leinster, Munster and Connacht*, 1950

Leaded Fanlight, Merrion Square

The delicate problems of the family of the first great Shavian were most delicately handled in the Abbey Theatre play, The Shaws of Synge Street, *by John*

O'Donovan, a contemporary Dubliner and Shavian of note, and the young George Bernard, or George Versus Bernard as J. P. Hackett had it, in an interesting study of Shaw, could, as he brooded over his and his family's problems in Synge Street, have heard the racket of the Terenure tram sailing past at Kelly's Corner; at which famous crossroads he would have mounted, and dismounted, from that same noble vehicle, going to and coming from the city centre.

Once, on the top of the Terenure tram, Lennox Robinson, playwright and a director of the Abbey Theatre, a tall, thin man and leaning like the Tower of Pisa, comically upset all the other passengers by elaborately capturing a butterfly that had found its way into the conveyance. He gently captured it, released it through a window, and announced :

If you had only a few hours to live you would not want to spend your lifetime on top of the Terenure tram.

On the top of the Terenure tram (it's a motorbus today), Thomas MacDonagh saw, before revolution and tragedy claimed him, a comic vision :

> A sailor sitting in a tram –
> A face that winces in the wind –
> That sees and knows me what I am,
> That looks through courtesy and sham
> And sees the good and bad behind –
> He is not God to save or damn,
> Thank God, I need not wish him blind.
>
> Calvin and Chaucer I saw today
> Come into the Terenure car:
> Certain I am that it was they,
> Though someone may know them here and say
> What different men they are.

I know their pictures – and there they sat,
And passing the Catholic church at Rathgar
Calvin took off his hat
And blessed himself, and Chaucer at that
Chuckled and looked away.

from *The Poetical Works of Thomas MacDonagh*

Synge Street (it is not called after the playwright) is as much or more renowned to Dubliners because it contains a famous school run by the Irish Christian Brothers as because it contains the birthplace of Bernard Shaw. Shaw was born in 1856, at number 33.

Shaw, like James Joyce, was the son of a drunkard, but, unlike Joyce, he did not emulate the parent. Shaw senior, between trips to the boozer, found time to be a snob; here in Synge Street he found the young George Bernard playing with a friend, and, on discovering that the playmate's father kept a shop in which he sold nails, he informed his son that it was dishonourable to associate with people who were in trade. Shaw senior owned a flour mill.

Adrian MacLoughlin, *Guide to Historic Dublin*, 1979

§

Michael Moran was born about 1794 off Blackpitts, in the Liberties of Dublin, in Faddle Alley. A fortnight after birth he went stone blind from illness, and became thereby a blessing to his parents, who were soon able to send him to rhyme and beg at street corners and at the bridges over the Liffey. They may well have wished that their quiver were full of such as he, for, free from the interruption of sight, his mind turned every movement of the days and every change of public passion into rhyme or quaint saying . . .

. . . when the fruit of his meditations did not ripen well, or when the crowd called for something more solid, he would recite or sing a metrical tale or ballad of saint or martyr or of biblical adventure. He would stand at a street corner, and when a crowd had gathered would begin in some such fashion as follows (I copy the record of one who knew him): – 'Gather round me, boys, gather round me. Boys, am I standin' in puddle? Am I standin' in wet?' Thereon several boys would cry, 'Ah, no! yez not! yer in a nice dry place. Go on with *Saint Mary*; go on with *Moses*' – each calling for his favourite tale . . .

The best-known of his religious tales was *Saint Mary of Egypt*, a long poem of exceeding solemnity, condensed from the much longer work of a certain Bishop Coyle. It told how an Egyptian harlot, Mary by name, followed pilgrims to Jerusalem in pursuit of her trade, and then, on finding herself withheld from entering the Temple by supernatural interference, turned penitent, fled to the desert and spent the remainder of her life in solitary penance. When at last she was at the point of death, God sent Bishop Zosimus to hear her confession, and, with the help of a lion, whom He sent also, dig her grave. The poem has the intolerable cadence of the eighteenth century at its worst, but was so popular and so often called for that Moran was nicknamed Zosimus, and by that name is he remembered. He had also a poem of his own called *Moses*, which went a little nearer poetry without going very near. But he could ill brook solemnity, and before long parodied his own verses in the following raga-muffin fashion:

In Egypt's land, contagious to the Nile,
King Pharoah's daughter went to bathe in style.
She took her dip, then walked unto the land,
To dry her royal pelt she ran along the strand.
A bulrush tripped her, whereupon she saw

A smiling babby in a wad of straw.
She tuk it up, and said with accents mild,
'Tare-and-agers, girls, which av yez owns the child.'

In April, 1846, word was sent to the priest that Michael Moran was dying. He found him at 15 (now 14½) Patrick Street, on a straw bed, in a room full of ragged ballad-singers come to cheer his last moments. After his death, the ballad-singers, with many fiddles and the like, came again and gave him a fine wake, each adding to the merriment whatever he knew in the way of rann, tale, old saw or quaint rhyme. He had had his day, had said his prayers and made his Confession, and why should they not give him a hearty send-off? The funeral took place the next day. A good party of his admirers and friends got into the hearse with the coffin, for the day was wet and nasty. They had not gone far when one of them burst out with, 'It's cruel cowld, isn't it?' 'Garra', replied another, 'we'll all be as stiff as the corpse when we get to the berrin'-ground.' 'Bad cess to him', said a third; 'I wish he'd held out another month until the weather got dacent.' A man called Carroll thereupon produced a half-pint of whiskey, and they all drank to the soul of the departed. Unhappily, however, the hearse was overweighted, and they had not reached the cemetery before the spring broke, and the bottle with it . . .

So William Butler Yeats on Patrick Moran, or Zosimus, the Last of the Gleemen, in a style that Brendan Behan once argued to me was both Protestant and patronizing. It was never such good fortune for the poor to have blind children, nor does the common speech of Dublin seem there to be faithfully echoed. Yet Yeats moving then in The Celtic Twilight *(1893) was a very young man searching for a folk-tradition and, by his own admission, for a prose-style.*

The explosive emergence of Brendan Behan was one of the most interesting of the phenomena of Dublin in the Fifties. In so far as he owed anything to anybody it was not to the Abbey Theatre nor the pundits of the Palace Bar but to his own family background, strongly nationalist, to the streets and the pubs of Dublin and the people on and in them, to the old Queen's Variety Theatre and, mayhap, even to the old Torch Theatre in Capel Street, and to Dion Boucicault to whom Seán O'Casey was also indebted. For the common speech of Dublin, Brendan, and small praise to him, had a faultless ear : as may be seen or heard from this encounter in a Dublin pub with Granny Grunt and Granny Growl and Chuckles and other citizens of note.

SHOUTING, MALE and FEMALE, likewise SCREECHES and ROARS

SHOUT. Granny Grunt, your blood's worth bottling.

ROAR. Me life on you, Granny Grunt.

SCREECH. A noble call, now, you have ma'am.

CHUCKLES. Granny Grunt, nominate your noble call.

GRANNY GRUNT. I call on the Granny Growl. Mrs Growl, ma'am, Maria Concepta, if I call you by your first name.

GRANNY GROWL. [*With dignity*] Certainly, Teresa Avila, to be sure.

CHUCKLES. Get something to lubricate your tonsils first.

[*Shouts*] More gargle there.

GRANNY GROWL. God bless you, me son.

GRANNY GRUNT. May the giving hand never falter.

1st VOICE. Up the Republic!

2nd VOICE. Up Everton!

3rd VOICE. Up the lot of yous.

[*Drinks are handed around*]

CHUCKLES. Did everyone get their gargle?
  [*Shouts of assent*]
CHUCKLES. Well, Granny Growl, give us your song.
  Carry on with the coffin . . . the corpse'll walk.
GRANNY GROWL and CHORUS. [*Sings*]
Get me down me petticoat and hand me down me
  shawl,
Get me down me petticoat, for I'm off to the Linen
  Hall
He was a quare one, fol de doo ah gow a dat,
He was a quare one, I tell you.

If you go to the Curragh Camp, ask for Number
  Nine,
You'll see three squaddies standing there,
And the best-looking one is mine.
He was a quare one . . . etc.

If he joined the Army under a false name,
To do me for me money,
It's his ould one's all to blame.
He was a quare one . . . etc.

If you put them to the war, out there to fight the
  Boers,
Will you try and hould the Dublins back
See the Bogmen go before.
He was a quare one . . . etc.

My love is on the ocean and me darling's on the sea,
My love he was a darling chap
Though he left me fixed this way.
He was a quare one . . . etc.

GRANNY GROWL. [*Sobs a bit*] Me tired husband, poor
  ould Paddins, he was shot in the Dardanelles.
GRANNY GRUNT. [*Sympathetically*] And a most
  painful part of the body to be shot.

[69]

GRANNY GROWL. And me first husband was et be the Ashantees. All they found of him was a button and a bone.

GRANNY GRUNT. God's curse to the hungry bastards.

GRANNY GROWL. But still an' all, ma'am, what business had he going near them. Me second husband had more sense. He stopped in the militia, and never went further than the Curragh for a fortnight.

GRANNY GRUNT. Maria Concepta, do you remember when we used to wait on them coming off the train at Kingsbridge and they after getting their bounty money, and waiting in on the station to be dismissed.

GRANNY GROWL. 'Deed and I do, Teresa Avila, and me provoked sergeant, he was an Englishman, would let a roar that'd go through you.

ANGEL. [*A visiting Englishman: in an NCO's roar*] Ri . . ght! To yore respective workhouses, pore'ouses and 'ore'ouses . . . d . . . iss . . . miss!

GRANNY GRUNT. That's the very way he used to shout. It used to thrill me through me boozem.

GRANNY GROWL. Poor ould Paddins, me tired husband . . .

Brendan Behan, The Big House, 1957

Dublin, being as it is, we could take a break for balladry. From some time in the nineteenth century, perhaps:

Come single belle and beau, to me now pay attention,
And love, I'll plainly show, is the divil's own invention:
For once in love I fell with a maiden's smiles
    bewitching,
Miss Henrietta Bell down in Captain Phibbs's kitchen.
Ritooral, etc.

At the age of seventeen I was tied unto a grocer,
Not far from Stephen's Green where Miss Bell for tea
    would go, sir.
Her manners were so free, she set my heart a-twitching,
She invited me to tea, down in Captain Phibbs's
    kitchen.
Ritooral, etc.

Next Sunday being the day, we were to have the flare-
    up,
I dressed myself quite gay, and I frizzed and oiled my
    hair up,
As the Captain had no wife, he had gone out a bitchin',
So we kicked up high life, below-stairs in the kitchen.
Ritooral, etc.

Just as the clock struck six we sat down to the table.
She handed tea and cakes, I ate while I was able.
I ate cakes, drank punch and tea, till my side had got a
    stitch in,
And the hours flew quick away, while coortin' in the
    kitchen.
Ritooral, etc.

With my arms around her waist, I kissed, she hinted
    marriage:
To the door in dreadful haste came Captain Phibbs's
    carriage.
Her looks told me full well at the moment she was
    wishin'
That I'd get out to hell, or somewhere from the
    kitchen.
Ritooral, etc.

She flew up off my knees, full five feet up or higher,
And, over head and heels, threw me slap into the
    fire.

My new Repealer's coat, that I bought from Mr
    Stitchen,
And a thirty-shilling note went to blazes in the
    kitchen.
Ritooral, etc.

I grieved to see my duds, all besmeared with smoke
    and ashes,
When a tub of dirty suds right in my face she dashes.
As I lay flat on the floor the water she kept pitchin',
Till the footman broke the door and marched down
    into the kitchen.
Ritooral, etc.

When the Captain came downstairs, though he seen
    my situation,
In spite of all my prayers I was marched off to the
    station.
For me they'd take no bail, tho' to get home I was
    itchin',
But I had to tell the tale of how I came into the
    kitchen.
Ritooral, etc.

I said she did invite me, but she gave a flat denial.
For assault she did indict me and I was sent for trial.
She swore I robbed the house, in spite of all her
    screechin'
So I six months went round the rack for coortin' in
    the kitchen.
Ritooral, etc.

*Nor would it seem possible to exclude the ballad that gave
its name, without the apostrophe, to a curious class of a
novel:*

Tim Finnegan lived in Walkin Street, a gentleman
    Irish, mighty odd.
He had a tongue both rich and sweet, and to rise in
    the world he carried a hod.
Now Tim had a sort of a tipplin' way, with a love of
    the liquor he was born,
And to help him on with his work each day, he'd a
    drop of the craythur every morn.

CHORUS

    Whack fol the da, dance to your partner,
    Welt the flure, your trotters shake.
    Wasn't it the truth I told you,
    Lots of fun at Finnegan's Wake.

*The bogman, or the culchie coming from Kiltimagh or
simply out of the woods, finds his way to Dublin, and
beyond it to Liverpool which is very very close to many
Dublin people. Had the Beatles, now, not a sort of a
decayed Dublin accent?*

In the merry month of May from my home I started,
Left the girls of Tuam nearly broken-hearted,
Saluted father dear, kissed my darling mother,
Drank a pint of beer my grief and tears to smother.
Then off to reap the corn, and leave where I was born,
I cut a stout blackthorn to banish ghost and goblin.
In a brand new pair of brogues I rattled o'er the bogs
And frightened all the dogs on the Rocky Road to
    Dublin.

CHORUS

One, two, three, four, five, hunt the hare and turn her,
Down the rocky road and all the way to Dublin.
Whack fol-lol-de-ra.

[73]

In Mullingar that night I rested limbs so weary,
Started by daylight, next mornin' light and airy,
Took a drop of the pure to keep my heart from
    sinkin',
That's the Paddy's cure when he's on for drinkin'.
To see the lasses smile, laughing all the while
At my curious style, 'twould set your heart a-bubblin'.
They asked if I was hired, the wages I required,
Till I was almost tired of the rocky road to Dublin.

In Dublin next arrived I thought it such a pity
To be so soon deprived a view of that fine city.
Then I took a stroll all among the quality,
My bundle it was stole in a neat locality.
Something crossed my mind, then I looked behind,
No bundle could I find upon my stick a wobblin'.
Enquirin' for the rogue, they said my Connacht
    brogue,
Wasn't much in vogue on the rocky road to Dublin.

From there I got away my spirits never failin',
Landed on the quay as the ship was sailin'.
Captain at me roared, said that no room had he
When I jumped aboard: a cabin found for Paddy
Down among the pigs. I played some funny rigs,
Danced some hearty jigs, the water round me bubblin':
Then off to Holyhead, I wished myself was dead,
Or, better far instead, on the rocky road to Dublin.

The boys of Liverpool, when we safely landed,
Called myself a fool, I could no longer stand it.
Blood began to boil, temper I was losin',
Poor old Erin's Isle they began abusin'.
Hurrah my soul, says I, my shillelagh I let fly,
Some Galway boys were by, saw I was a hobble-in.
Then with a loud hurray, they joined in the affray,
We quickly cleared the way from the rocky road to
    Dublin.

Trinity College

'Give me but the making of the ballads, and I care not who should make the laws of a nation,' is an apophthegm attributed to Chatham and Voltaire, but in reality the words of Fletcher of Saltoun.

From the days of 'Lillibulero', a war of ballads was waged between the rival races and parties of Ireland. 'The Wearing of the Green' was answered by 'Croppies, Lie Down', and the 'Shan Van Voght', by 'Protestant Boys.' Both sexes followed the craft of street ballad-singing.

Dublin had long been famous for its vocal powers in this line; and it is recorded of Goldsmith that, when a sizar, he wrote some of these ballads, and 'creeping within dark shadows of the ill-lighted streets' would watch the effect produced on the motley audience. Lever has also been known to glide from Trinity College at night on a kindred mission.

Many of the old Dublin ballads were coarse and scurrilous, which tried to make up in bitterness for their lack of humour; but occasionally were found real gems of passionate feeling, sparkling with native wit and possessing the true ring. In the composition of many of these ballads Lever was directly concerned. He saturated his mind in such portions of the ballad literature of Ireland as deserved attention and on one occasion . . . 'having hired the uniform and accoutrements of the prototype of Rhoudlum – an historical personage still remembered in Dublin, and introduced in his novel, *The Knight of Gwynne* – he went the length of singing, in the most frequented part of Dublin, a political ballad of his own, judged to be too strong by the regular professionals. A great row ensued, but a party of fellow-students were at hand to rescue the amateur singer, and bear him off in triumph . . . The glorious days of Dublin ballad-singing were before the new policeman (i.e. The Peeler) came to say: 'Move on!' . . .

Lever ran some risk of popular chastisement from the freedom with which he . . . used favourite names:

> O, Dublin City, there is no doubting
> Bates every city upon the say:
> 'Tis there you'd hear O'Connell spouting,
> And see Lady Morgan making tay.
> For 'tis the capital of the finest nation
> With charming peasantry on a fruitful sod,
> Fighting like divils for conciliation
> And hating each other for the love of God.
>
> W. J. Fitzpatrick, *The Life of Charles Lever*, 1884

Ringsend

But back for a moment to that Ringsend that was once the port for Dublin: from which the Ousel galley once sailed to be captured by Barbary corsairs, to be recaptured by her own crew who then robbed the robbers and sailed back to Ringsend: laden down with loot which went to build the old Commercial Buildings in Dame Street, with a Dickensian courtyard and a greystone plaque showing a galley in full sail. There was for a time a pub called the Ousel Galley, formerly the Bodega, and a meeting-place of the literati. All gone now, eaten up by the new enormous Central Bank building.

Once upon a time Brendan Behan and a companion who, as they say, married into Ringsend, had a dispute with the friend's in-laws in a Ringsend pub. The dispute developed into violent dimensions and the two heroes (both of them are now gone to God) were compelled to wade to safety across the limitless strand of Sandymount where the tide was running but fortunately not near the full. Next day Brendon, disguised in bruises and sticking-plaster, said to me, in simple explanation: 'They're a peculiar crowd of savages in Ringsend.'

§

Oliver St John Gogarty, poet, wit, surgeon, doctor, friend of Yeats and Moore, sometime suffering friend of James Joyce, cast kinder eyes on that place when, after perhaps a surfeit of Tolstoy, he wrote:

> I will live in Ringsend
> With a red-headed whore,
> And the fan-light gone in
> Where it lights the halldoor;
> And listen each night
> For her querulous shout,
> As at last she streels in
> And the pubs empty out.
> To soothe that wild breast
> With my old-fangled songs,
> Till she feels it redressed
> From inordinate wrongs,
> Imagined, outrageous,

Preposterous wrongs,
Till peace at last comes,
Shall be all I will do,
Where the little lamp blooms
Like a rose in the stew;
And up the back garden
The sound comes to me
Of the lapsing, unsoilable,
Whispering sea.

from *Others to Adorn*, 1938

On the Dublin that bred Gogarty, Ulick O'Connor writes in his admirable biographical study Oliver St John Gogarty: A Poet and his Times *(1964)*:

One quality which would have struck a visitor to Edwardian Dublin was the air of indolence about the place. There were no factory chimneys to blacken the landscape. The atmosphere was leisurely, divorced from the pace of an industrial city. There was an almost Latin disregard for time, which may have had its origin in the strong Catholic element among the people. The sea air, too, induced alternate moods of lethargy and elation, typical of maritime climates. The presence of the university and the garrison contributed to the leisurely mood; the gowned students sauntering out for a talk and coffee into the centre of the city, the colourful cavalry strolling through the streets with jingling spurs in the early afternoon suggested a life that was not tied to the routine of the counting-house, or the tyranny of the clock.

The pace of life left plenty of time for tongue-wagging. A facet common to all citizens was the feeling for words. The poor had the Gaelic flair for language as 'fully flavoured as a nut or apple' that their forebears from the country had before they came to live in the city. O'Casey's dialogue has shown how the imagery of Synge's peasant folk survived among the Dublin poor, but transmuted in the crucible of tenement life with overtones of sarcasm and derision . . .

This passion for conversation obtained at all levels. The Chief Secretary's Lodge, the Viceregal Lodge, the tables of judges and doctors in Fitzwilliam and Merrion Squares, the houses of the dons, were meeting-places for the best talkers in the town. The middle classes had their musical evenings with songs, monologues, instrumental performances, dramatic recitals, and talk in between, the last item taking up more than a fair proportion of the time.

The Countess of Fingall, who introduced Edward VII to Father Healy of Little Bray, a famous talker of his day, has recalled the almost compulsive talking habits of the Dublin of that time: 'I cannot count the wits and story-tellers of those days; you used to see men buttonholing one another at street corners in Dublin, to tell stories and roaring with laughter over them . . .'

Oliver St John Gogarty commenced the torrent of talk in his book As I was Going Down Sackville Street: A Phantasy in Fact *(1937), with a most vivid portrait of a celebrated Dublin character : Endymion.*

Quaintly he came raiking out of Molesworth Street into Kildare Street, an odd figure moidered by memories, and driven mad by dreams which had overflowed into life, making him turn himself into a merry mockery of all he had once held dear. He wore a tail-coat over white cricket trousers which were caught in at the ankles by a pair of cuffs. A cuff-like collar sloped upwards to keep erect a little sandy head, crowned by a black bowler some sizes too small. An aquiline nose high in the arch gave a note of distinction to a face all the more pathetic for its plight. Under his left arm he carried two sabres in shining scabbards of patent leather. His right hand grasped a hunting-crop such as whippers-in use for hounds. His small, sharp blue eyes took in the ash-dark façade, topped by a green-white-and-orange flag, of that which had been the Duke of Leinster's town house; but it held the Senate now . . .

What were the memories he 'represented' by his accoutrements and his dress? What turned him into his present lunatic condition? To answer these questions we must go back to the days when the great Lord Lieutenant, the Earl Cadogan, held state in the Phoenix Park. That Viceroy, hearing of an act of gallantry which had cost the man his reason, sought him out, and finding that he was but slightly touched gave him the run of the viceregal grounds, with their pageants of state and their cricket matches. He was but slightly 'touched', for he had wit enough to realise his trouble. So, when his doctor told him that his mental disability was likely to become progressive, but that he would never be violently unbalanced, he remarked: 'Endymion, whom the moon loved: a lunatic . . .'

So Endymion he became . . . the sabres are his cavalry escort, for he must have been impressed by the cavalcade of sixty well-mounted troopers who attended the viceregal carriages; and the cricket flannels – his memories of summer evenings on the smooth pitch; the whip, his runs in winter with the staghounds of the Ward. All gone now; alive only in memory and regret, those peaceful, prosperous days when life was fair and easy and man's thoughts were the thoughts of sportsmen . . .

As Tom Corkery has elsewhere remarked, there are constant lamentations that the celebrated Dublin characters are vanishing, or have vanished: and in these

times of stereotype and television there may be truth in
that, even if the lamentations are sometimes made by
men who are themselves, most undeniably, original
characters.

My friend, the late Dominic O'Riordan, was a Kerryman, but his great amiable nature and his poetic mind,
('God's procreant waters flowing about your mind . . .')
made him a memorable addition to the life of Dublin.

It is a proud thing to be able to recall that day when
he paid elegiac honour to one who was the most Dublin
of all Dublinmen.

Coming from a great-hearted Kerryman, the lines are
generous and all gold :

> No young Michael Angelo, he,
> Painting on ceilings gaiety,
> For painting was his family trade.
> When police on genius made a raid
> And into prison hurried a fighter,
> Goliath Behan came out a roaring writer,
> True brother of Rabelais O'Suilleabháin:
> Those tempestuous gentlemen,
> Young with Marlowe and Dylan Thomas,
> In spring extravagance of promise:
> Scattering words as God did stars,
> Through frothy exuberance of bars,
> A hostage of too much talent,
> Ribald, blatant, innocent,
> Sending language on a spree,
> Drunk with Dublin's imagery:
> Surely Evelyn Waugh will strangle,
> When he hears the Ould Triangle
> Sung by all the heavenly host,
> With Brendan Behan soloist.
> Oh the Captains and the Kings
> Oh my Behan and my Dublin long ago.

I remember him riding the air,
A mixture of Puck and the Goban Saor,
Through Grafton Street of an early day,
With ruffled shirt and hair astray
Respectable gents and frightened aunts
Held tightly to their briefs and pants,
Lest their bowels might be disturbed
Or their complacency perturbed
Hearing genius roaring by
On words of love and obscenity,
They'd whisper 'He never got his Ph.D.
From U.C.D. or T.C.D.
Nor did he believe in L.S.D.
Which means you know Laus Semper Deo.'

Improper words are never adorning
And not during coffee of a
tête-à-tête morning,
Like scarperer, joxer, fluther, brother,
Hould your hour and have another,
O the Captains and the Kings
O my Behan, O my Dublin long ago.

Now the dying hag has sung,
Her *caoine* for the very young
And Russell Street and neighbour and nation
Fallen in *gombeen* speculation:
Scattered and transformed hermits
In Kimmages and Ballyfermots,
But I'm sure he'll have his say
And sing a stave with Rabelais,
And the voice of God will thunder
Behan, give us another number,
And the gates of hell will open
By kind permission of Mr Behan.

How could he be happy where
All the lost were not gathered there:
And the ould Triangle will jingle jangle
Along the bars and canals of heaven.
Oh the Captains and the Kings
Oh my Brendan, oh my Dublin long ago.

(previously unpublished)

The Hills

The hills, or mountains to the south of the city, so close in mileage, so remote in secluded peace, are very much part of the life of Dublin. They fill in the view at the end of many a street: notably, say, as you look along Lower Rathmines Road or from Merrion Square along Fitz-william Street and Square.

Hidden in odd hollows of the hills are cold deep tarns: the one nearest to the city, Loch Bray, is here celebrated by the scholar and historical novelist, Standish James O'Grady (1846–1928), a sort of foundational member of the Irish Literary Renaissance.

Now Memory, false spendthrift Memory,
Disloyal treasure-keeper of the Soul,
This vision change shall never wring from thee
Nor wasteful years effacing as they roll,
O steel-blue lake, high-cradled in the hills!
O sad waves, filled with little sobs and cries!
White glistening shingle, hiss of mountain rills,
And granite-hearted walls blotting the skies,
Shine, sob, gleam, gloom for ever! O, in me
Be what you are in nature – a recess
To sadness dedicate, and mystery,
Withdrawn, afar, in the soul's wilderness.
Still let my thoughts leaving the worldly roar
Like pilgrims wander on thy haunted shore.

from Hugh Art O'Grady, *Standish James O'Grady:*
the Man and the Writer, 1929

Within my own memory there lived in a cottage by Loch
Bray a kindly man called Doak whose wife kept a tea-
shop and a visitor's book that was a truly remarkable
record of great names from the high period at the beginning
of the century, including that of John Millington Synge,
who much loved these hills, and who came here to meet his
lady-love.

Doak is dead and his wife, the cottage closed, and
God knows where the book is. The lake, or rather the two
lakes, upper and lower, still `cast cold eyes on the high
skies that Synge said were over Ireland and 'the lonesome
mornings with birds crying on the bog'.

But once again to Ulick O'Connor writing in his
Gogarty book about the hills beloved by him and every
other Dublinman or Dubliner :

The natural surroundings and architectural layout of
Dublin also had their influence on the personality of
the people. Dublin is a city, as George Moore said
pleasantly about it, 'wandering between hill and sea'.

In the Dubliner's mind is the knowledge that he can always get to sandy beaches, or goat-paths in lonely hills in less than a half-hour. Dublin Bay with its long beaches stretches for almost forty miles, and behind it lies a crescent of hills each merging into one another, with soft names like Kilmashogue, the Feather Bed, the Sally Gap, the Silver Spears.

The architects who laid the city out in the eighteenth century were always conscious of the natural beauty surrounding it. They crowned their public buildings with green domes to merge with the sky and the tidal waters of the Liffey. Between the tall houses and wide streets they framed panoramas of the hills, so that on clear days vistas of green and gold strike the eye at the end of a street or square. They bent stone until it accommodated the clouds and knew exactly how to use hill and sky against an urban background.

Always in Gogarty there was a pastoral awareness of nature, exceptional in one so deeply involved in the stream of city life. The hills and beaches of the city were his escape hatches to beauty, when his professional career and social activities began to limit his free time. He would roar up the hills in his Rolls at lunch-hour, or gallop on the beach before breakfast in order to nourish the persistent demand in him for the prospect of nature.

The situation of the city helped satisfy this craving in his being. As a young man after he had given up cycling he spent many hours roaming the silent hills, the silence broken, as Pádraic Colum remembers, by the chant of Gogarty reciting ode after ode of Pindar; or swimming in the sea along Dublin Bay. Hardy as Vikings, he and his poet friends gave the weak northern sun the same adulation as the sun-kissed Greeks, defying the cold winds and stinging salt water, to feel on their bodies as young pagans might, the caress of its life-giving rays.

> Lords of the morning, since you set
> Within this ancient heart
> The flame that burnt my youth away
> And set my life apart,
> I bring you in this urn of truth
> The dust-white ashes of my youth . . .

wrote one of Gogarty's swimming companions, the poet Seamus O'Sullivan, who felt the forces of nature shaping his manhood, though he like Gogarty had been born and bred in the heart of the city.

Ulick O'Connor, *Oliver St John Gogarty:
A Poet and his Times*, 1964

Though time effaces memory and griefs the bosom
    harden,
I'll ne'er forget, where'er I be that day at Killenarden;
For there, while fancy revelled wide, the summer's
    day flew o'er me;
The friends I loved were at my side, and Irish fields
    before me.

The road was steep; the pelting showers had cooled
    the sod beneath us;
And there were lots of mountain flowers, a garland to
    unwreath us.
Far, far, below the landscape shone with wheat and
    new-mown meadows,
And as o'erhead the clouds flew on, beneath swept on
    their shadows.

O friends, beyond the Atlantic's foam there may be
    noble mountains,
And in our new far western home green fields and
    brighter fountains;

But, as for me, let time destroy all dreams, but this
    one pardon,
And barren memory long enjoy that day on Killenarden.
from Irish Minstrelsy, ed. H. Halliday Sparling, 1888

*The poet singing his memories of a happy day on the hills
above Dublin was not even a Dublinman, but a man who
was born in Oldcastle, County Meath, under the shadow
of the Loughcrew hills, in 1829: Charles Graham
Halpine. He died in New York in 1868. His father was
editor of the Dublin* Evening Mail *no longer with us and,
to quote H. Halliday Sparling in his* Irish Minstrelsy
(1888),

an unrelenting foe of the popular cause; but the son
became associated with the Young Irelanders, and was
compelled to seek an asylum over the water. There he
obtained abundant employment and under the name of
Miles O'Reilly wrote many popular anti-secession
lyrics. He attained the rank of Brigadier-General
during the War of Secession.

§

There is nothing further worthy of notice along the
main road until we reach the small group of cottages
called Jobstown, where we take the turn to the left,
known as the Killenarden road, up the steep slope of
Knockannavea Mountain or Tallaght Hill. The road
becomes rougher as it ascends higher up the mountain-
side, and we pass between high hedgebanks of haw-
thorn and furze, with occasional growths of fern and
the graceful lusmore or foxglove.

Emerging, at length, from the enclosing hedges, our
view extends over the plain and Bay of Dublin, while
to the eastward will be seen Mount Pelier, Kilmashogue,
the Three Rocks and Killakee Mountains; and con-

tinuing our journey, near the top of the road we meet, on the left, a narrow lane, said to be portion of an ancient track by which, in remote times, the dead were borne from the plains to be interred in the churchyards among these wild hills.

On the right will now be observed a picturesque little defile overgrown with furze and stunted woods, rising over the far side of which is the hill called Lugmore, an offshoot of Knockannavea. Extending away towards Dublin will be seen the wide Blessington road, and at times may be heard the shrill whistle of the steam tram echoing among the hills, its harshness agreeably softened by distance.

We now pass a small farmhouse in a somewhat exposed position, sheltered by a plantation of elder and thorn bushes, and shortly afterwards reach the summit of the mountain called Knockannavinidee, locally known as Killenarden Hill. The road here becomes a mere bridle-track through the furze, the turf springs under our feet, and the higher mountains to the southward come into view. Mount Pelier with its conspicuous ruin [the Hellfire Club] lies on her left; further to the southward is the great military road winding like a white ribbon across Killakee mountain; below it is the road from Bohernabreena through Piperstown, and due south the towering summit of Seechon.

After reaching the brow of the hill a small pond can be seen on the left; about half a mile beyond this pond the track runs beside a rough stone wall with a double line of barbed wire on top; keep along by this wall until it turns at a sharp angle to the left, and on the summit of the eminence to the right is Raheen Dhu, one of the most perfect raths to be found in the neighbourhood of Dublin . . .

Sixty-nine years ago Weston St John Joyce, son of P. W. Joyce, took that mountain walk and wrote about it in his classic The Neighbourhood of Dublin. *The steam tram has whistled its way, somewhat like Carlyle's Merovingian kings, into eternity, but the road, better surfaced nowadays, rises like the side of a house above Jobstown and, after reaching the brow of the hill the small pond will still be seen on the left. The view to the east and into the heart of the hills is unchanged; but if you look behind, as Lot's daughter was advised not to do, the inexorable parallel lines of suburbia pursue you.*

But in the Thirties and into the Forties, Dr George A. Little went out time and again from Rathgar by Terenure Cross and Templeogue and Tallaght and along the road towards Blessington and Poulaphuca and Baltinglass as far as Jobstown Inn and the road up Killenarden. This was the mountainy man he went up to meet, and to listen to . . .

Malachi Horan sat in what I was to discover was his favourite place – the right hand of the ingle-nook. Over his head a curved tree-trunk forms a natural and elegant lintel-arch to his hearth. On his face met the light from the window and that from the fire . . . A square face of great power, eyes grey-green beneath a penthouse of bushy white brows; lips so firm set as to be almost immobile; skin tanned and wrinkled as a late betided strand; woolly-white hair and sidewhiskers – a face set to the world, or to a purpose, but one which yet could smile more easily than frown . . .

From the talk of this old mountainy man came Dr Little's book Malachi Horan Remembers *(1943), a rare look into the ways of the past in the Dublin mountains. This was Malachi speaking:*

'I was born in this house ninety-five years ago come

Martinmas . . . My father came to this place from Landenstown in the County of Kildare sometime before the rebellion of 1798. This farm was all furze then. But he killed the hill, that is cleared it of whins and heather . . . he covered the furze with sand and yellow clay so that they rotted. The next year he ploughed them in. It was the old wooden plough he used, the same as I used after. They could not stand to the work like the steel plough. But a good man with good beasts could do plenty with them. It was oxen we used. Gentle beasts they were, and as kind as silk to work . . .

'I remember my father (God be good to him) telling of how Patrick Lawlor – a decent poor man enough – came by his end. It was about the year of '98. Lawlor was as poor as a fiddler's kit. One day he went on some message to a big house up in Brittas beyond. The window by the door was open, and Lawlor saw a half-ounce of tobacco in a box and three halfpence on a table and it beside a window. He whipped them up and stuck them in his pocket. Frightened by what he had done, he took his leg-bail. But, troth, he was not long on his keeping before they followed and took him. He was found guilty. They bound him in chains and hanged him on a gibbet below there on Killenarden. A mournful sound, they say, he used to make and him swinging in the wind – God rest him! his sin was not so great. About forty years ago the chains that bound him were dug up at the spot where the gallows stood. They were used after to shoe a slide-cart that they had for shifting stones.

'When I was a lad I knew a man myself that fought in '98. He was 106 years of age when he died. Bill Donacha was his name. He was a dark small man and very powerful. He had his farm at Sandybanks beyond at Brittas.

'"I killed but one man in the whole of my life, and him only when he tried for mine," Donocha would be always explaining.'

So close to the city the hills hold their own dark stories. It is not all beauty. Malachi Horan told Dr Little that

'there was an old man named Boylan who lived in Killenarden. He could not keep his mouth shut. He went about saying that they were hanging men for nothing. One of the magistrates heard this and said that the dignity of the bench would have to be upheld; so they took Neddy Boylan, son of the old man, and hanged him, although they knew him innocent. They said that as he was not content to live by English law that he had better die by it.'

For John Ryan, growing up in Dublin suburbia, and surveying the scene at the mid-century, the hills came down to meet the growing city :

Roads here [Rathgar] seem to end in mountains, and it appears to be not the streets and houses that are thrusting towards the country, but the hills (like earthy glaciers) that are seeping inexorably back into the genteel mellowed suburb. The whole area, including Brighton Square West, where Joyce was born, may, arguably, be the most perfectly intact, homogeneous, early Victorian, urban landscape we have. The architecture is chaste and nearer the Prince Regent than the Prince Consort; for the hand of the Dublin tradesman and master builder (recalling earlier and better disciplines), could not readily fashion things that were alien both to taste and eye. They were men with, perhaps, memories of their own fathers creating Mountjoy and Merrion Squares and, therefore, well-grounded in the canon of the Georgian aesthetic.

Our house was on Orwell Road, which begins at the intersection of Rathgar Avenue and Rathgar Road, the latter a truly noble thoroughfare, graciously wide, running like a lofty geometric statement, through a charming chance medley of structures great and small – until it runs out of ideas and just allows itself to be swallowed by a confusion of lesser, meaner roads and streets.

Remembering How We Stood, 1975

Robert Farren has said that a dream may be sweet in Wicklow Street as a dream in a Wicklow valley. John Synge had his vision of famous queens in one of the most wonderful of those valleys:

> Seven dog-days we let pass
> Naming Queens in Glenmacnass
> All the rare and royal names
> Wormy sheepskin yet retains:
> Etain, Helen, Maeve, and Fand,
> Golden Deirdre's tender hand;
> Bert, the big-foot, sung by Villon.
> Cassandra, Ronsard found in Lyon.
> Queens of Sheba, Meath, and Connaught,
> Coifed with crown, or gaudy bonnet;
> Queens whose finger once did stir men,
> Queens were eaten of fleas and vermin,
> Queens men drew like Mona Lisa,
> Or slew with drugs in Rome and Pisa.
> We named Lucrezia Crivelli,
> And Titian's lady with amber belly,
> Queens acquainted in learned sin,
> Jane of Jewry's slender shin:
> Queens who cut the boss of Glanna,
> Judith of Scripture, and Gloriana,
> Queens who wasted the East by proxy,
> Or drove the ass-cart, a tinker's doxy.

Yet these are rotten – I ask their pardon –
And we've the sun on rock and garden;
These are rotten, so you're the Queen
Of all are living, or have been.

Memories

*In the year of the Act of Union that never did much
succeed in uniting anybody with anybody else, the Parliament House in College Green had an interested young
English visitor :*

The House of Lords, decorated (if I remember) with
hangings representing the battle of the Boyne, was
nearly empty when we entered – an accident which
furnished to Lord Altamont the opportunity required
for explaining to us the whole course and ceremonial
of public business on ordinary occasions.

Gradually the House filled: beautiful women sat
intermingled amongst the peers . . . Then were
summoned to the bar – summoned for the last time –
the gentlemen of the House of Commons; in the van
of whom, and drawing all eyes upon himself, stood
Lord Castlereagh . . .

At which point in the order of succession came the
Royal Assent to the Union Bill, I cannot distinctly
recollect. But one thing I *do* recollect – that no audible
expression, no buzz, nor murmur, nor *susurrus* even,
testified the feelings which, doubtless, lay rankling
in many bosoms. Setting apart all public or patriotic
considerations, even then I said to myself, as I surveyed the whole assembly of ermined peers, 'How is it,
and by what unaccountable magic, that William Pitt
can have prevailed on all these hereditary legislators
and heads of patrician houses to renounce so easily,

with nothing worth the name of a struggle, and no reward worth the name of an indemnification, the very brightest jewel in their coronets? This morning they all rose from their couches Peers of Parliament, individual pillars of the realm, indispensable parties to every law that could pass. Tomorrow they will be nobody – men of straw – *terraefilii*.

'What madness has persuaded them to part with their birthright, and to cashier themselves and their children forever into mere titular Lords?' . . .

'You are all,' thought I to myself, 'a pack of vagabonds henceforward, and interlopers, with actually no more right to be here than myself. I am an intruder; so are you.' Apparently they thought so themselves: for, soon after this solemn *fiat* of Jove had gone forth, their lordships, having no farther title to their robes (for which I could not help wishing that a party of Jewish old-clothes men would at this moment have appeared and made a loud bidding), made what haste they could to lay them aside forever. The House dispersed much more rapidly than it had assembled . . .

One person only I remarked whose features were suddenly illuminated by a smile, a sarcastic smile, as I read it; which, however, might be all a fancy. It was Lord Castlereagh; who, at the moment when the irrevocable words were pronounced, looked with a penetrating glance amongst a party of ladies. His own wife was one of that party; but I did not discover the particular object on whom his smile had settled . . .

Collected Writings of Thomas de Quincey, ed. David
Masson, 1896

That was Thomas de Quincey remembering how, as a young man, he accompanied the young Lord Westport to Dublin and then to Connacht to the home of his father, Lord Altamont.

The Bedford Tower, Dublin Castle

VALE!
Around me the images of thirty years:
An ambush; pilgrims at the water-side;
Casement upon trial, half-hidden by the bars,
Guarded; Griffith staring in hysterical pride;
Kevin O'Higgins' countenance that wears
A gentle questioning look that cannot hide
A soul incapable of remorse or rest;
A revolutionary soldier kneeling to be blest;

An Abbot or Archbishop with an upraised hand
Blessing the Tricolour. 'This is not', I say,
'The dead Ireland of my youth, but an Ireland
The poets have imagined, terrible and gay.'
Before a woman's portrait suddenly I stand,
Beautiful and gentle in her Venetian way.
I met her all but fifty years ago
For twenty minutes in some studio.

Heart-smitten with emotion I sink down,
My heart recovering with covered eyes;
Wherever I had looked I had looked upon
My permanent or impermanent images:
Augusta Gregory's son; her sister's son,
Hugh Lane, 'onlie begetter' of all these;
Hazel Lavery living and dying, that tale
As though some ballad-singer had sung it all;

Mancini's portrait of Augusta Gregory,
'Greatest since Rembrandt', according to John Synge;
A great ebullient portrait certainly;
But where is the brush that could show anything
Of all that pride and that humility?
And I am in despair that time may bring
Approved patterns of women or of men
But not that selfsame excellence again.

My mediaeval knees lack health until they bend,
But in that woman, in that household where
Honour had lived so long, all lacking found.
Childless I thought, 'My children may find here
Deep-rooted things,' but never foresaw its end,
And now that end has come I have not wept;
No fox can foul the lair the badger swept –

(An image out of Spenser and the common tongue).
John Synge, I and Augusta Gregory, thought
All that we did, all that we said or sang
Must come from contact with the soil, from that
Contact everything Antaeus-like grew strong.
We three alone in modern times had brought
Everything down to that sole test again,
Dream of the noble and the beggar-man.

And here's John Synge himself, that rooted man,
'Forgetting human words', a grave deep face.
You that would judge me, do not judge alone
This book or that, come to this hallowed place
Where my friends' portraits hang and look thereon;
Ireland's history in their lineaments trace;
Think where man's glory most begins and ends,
And say my glory was I had such friends.

W. B. Yeats, 'The Municipal Gallery Revisited'

That 'hallowed place' is the Municipal Art Gallery in Parnell Square on the north side of the Liffey. It is as meaningful a place as we could choose from which to commence the final saunter in this city. It is linked with that aspect of the eighteenth century which the poet Yeats (just there celebrating his friends of a much later date) so much admired. The building was the town-house of the Earl of Charlemont, the commander-in-chief of the Irish Volunteers of 1892, a body that had seemed to guarantee for a brief period the existence of a sort of Irish nation. And the building is linked with London and the Tate Gallery through the controversy, now amicably, if partially resolved, over the ownership of the Hugh Lane pictures.

Across the roadway and enclosed by the railings of the Square is the splendid statuary by Oisín Kelly, celebrating another risen nation and taking its imagery, oddly perhaps, from the legend of the children of Lír: children into swans and, much later, swans into advanced geriatrics.

The railings of the Square also enclose the Lying-in Hospital; and at the corner, as we come, going southwards, down the slope, there is the Gate Theatre and the Rotunda (already mentioned), once a notable eighteenth-century assembly-hall, now the quite respectable Ambassador Cinema. Somewhere in between it suffered through a

*shadowy period as a cinema called the Roto into which,
it was jocosely said, admission could be procured by the
proferring of jam-pots.*

*But far from us be all such gutter-humour. A pause
for a moment at the Gate Theatre, and the origin of
Longford Productions:*

At Oxford [Edward Longford] didn't join a dramatic
society, but as a playgoer he was madly enthusiastic
as I was. In the big commercial New Theatre we
enjoyed the touring Macdona Players in Shaw;
separately we applauded the Irish Players from Dublin,
Maire O'Neill, Sara Allgood and Arthur Sinclair, and
we hardly realized that they were a split from the
original Abbey. On their opening night the Oxford
Irish Society booked seats in the stalls and there was a
mild sensation.

When the theatre orchestra struck up their suitable
Irish airs, 'Let Érin Remember', and so on, a crowd of
young men in dinner jackets, Edward included, sprang
to their feet as if for a national anthem. I didn't witness
the incident, but some English and less emotional Irish
thought it in very bad taste. Edward went to a party
given by the company in their theatrical digs in
Paradise Square, and Miss Allgood gave him a signed
photograph which he treasured . . .

Then in the Michaelmas Term something more
important happened to us in Oxford: J. B. Fagan gave
us a new theatre. It has now passed into theatrical
history, but it can't be repeated too often that the first
Oxford Playhouse was a small, ugly, uncomfortable
building where Fagan, the Irish actor, playwright,
producer and manager worked miracles . . .

*That was Christine, Lady Longford, one of the greatest
ladies ever to walk in Dublin, remembering in* Enter

Certain Players: Edward Mac Liammoir and the Gate
(1928–78).

*At the junction of Abbey Street and Marlborough Street,
the voice of Ria Mooney, whose friendship I was privileged
to enjoy, remembers the first production of* The Plough
and the Stars, *and her part in it as Rosie Redmond,
historic daughter of the town :*

At last the great night came, February 8th, 1926.
Everything was normal, no more excitement than actors
usually experience when they are about to appear in a
new play. When the show was over, I met Seán
O'Casey as he crossed the stage. He stopped for a
moment, and, unlike previous occasions, when his face
would be screwed up while he gazed out of his better
eye, there was a pale seriousness about our usually
animated author, and his face was calm. 'Thank you for
saving my play,' he said, and when I looked incredul-
ously at him, he added, 'I mean that.' Then he walked
away.

Quite honestly (and you may find this hard to
believe), I had reached twenty-three years of age
without knowing precisely what was meant by a
'prostitute'. I had certainly learned what prostitutes
looked like and how they dressed, by following the
advice I had been given, but that was as far as my
knowledge went. Without knowing exactly why, however, I felt very sorry for these young girls I had seen
in the lane. So when the Covey sneers at Rosie, and
says he is not 'goin' to take no reprimandin' from a
prostitute', I was so hurt that real tears came as I
rushed at him, crying: 'Yer no man! I'm a woman
anyway, an' I have me feelin's.'

I learnt a great deal about acting from this incident.
When, in later years, I gave exactly the same perform-
ance technically, and (so far as even those members of

the public who had seen it several times before could judge), the very same interpretation, it never again was really the same, because my total sympathy with the character had gone.

Technique, without feeling and concentration, is like Faith without Good Works: it is dead. When I had felt sympathy for the character, the audience felt it too, and so Rosie received understanding of her plight, when she might have aroused antagonism. That was, I suppose, what Seán meant when he thanked me for 'saving his play.'

from *George Spelvin's Theatre Book*, 1971

At the top of O'Connell Street and at the foot of the Parnell Monument is the appropriate place to quote Seán O'Casey remembering his boyhood as it was affected by the emotions all around him at the time of the funeral of Charles Stewart Parnell:

The brown coffin came along, the box that held all Ireland had, sailing, like a drab boat, over a tossing sea of heads, falling, rising, and sinking again, polished by the falling rain; flanked on the one hand by the dirty dribbling railway station, and by the fat and heavy-pillared front of St. Andrew's Church on the other; but few were going in to bow before the altar, or mutter a prayer for the repose of a pining soul in purgatory; for all were here, all were here, gazing at the brown coffin sailing along, like a drab boat, over a sea of tossing heads, falling, rising, and sinking again, polished by the falling rain, silent, the coffin went on, in the midst of the rolling drumbeat of the Dead March.

Ireland's uncrowned King is gone.

And a wail came from a voice in the crowd, keening, We shall lie down in sorrow, and arise sorrowing in the face of the morning; there is none left to guide us in the midst of our sorrow; sorrow shall follow us in all our ways; and our face shall never wear the veil of gladness. We shall never rejoice again as a strong man rejoiceth; for our Leader has vanished out of our sight . . .

An Ireland came into view, an Ireland shaped like a hearse, with a jet-black sky overhead, like a pall, tinged with a broad border of violet and purple where the sun had set for ever, silvered gently by the light of many cold and silent stars; and, in the midst of the jet-black sky, the pure white, set face of the dead chief rested, his ears shut dead to the wailing valour. Our uncrowned King of Ireland's gone!

A moving mass of lone white faces strained with anger, tight with fear, loose with grief, great grief, wandered round and round where the whiter face lay, set like a dimming pearl in the jet-black sky, violet-rimmed where the sun had set for ever, silvered softly by the dozing stars, sinking deeper into the darkness soon to forever hide the warm hope of Ireland waning.

Out of the east came a sound of cheering.

Joy is theirs, cried a voice from the wailing; overflowing joy, for they feel safe now, and their sun is rising; their table is spread and their wine is circling; lift your heads and you'll hear them cheering.

The English!

Seán O'Casey, *Pictures in the Hallway*, 1942

Compare this with the scene at the Christmas dinner in A Portrait of the Artist as a Young Man. *Or with Yeats:*

> Come gather round me Parnellites,
> Come praise our chosen man . . .

Monuments

How many monuments between here and that sad Robert
Emmet, by O'Connor, sheltering in the hedges in Stephen's
Green? Count them as you saunter.

A. Norman Jeffares writes in his biography of W. B.
Yeats:

Unfortunately the need for reconciling Anglo–Irish
and Nationalist was complicated by the religious
differences which underlie Irish politics; and Yeats had
not contributed to the reconciliation by the speech
which he made in the Senate in June 1925, on the
subject of divorce. The Free State Government was
introducing measures to prohibit divorce, and in his
speech Yeats regarded this measure as 'grossly oppressive' to the Protestant minority, who were as much part
of Ireland as the majority, who had written most of its
modern literature, and who had created the best of
its political thought. It was a tactless speech.

For instance, he introduced the private lives of the
three public figures, Nelson, O'Connell and Parnell,
whose statues decorate Dublin's main street, of whom
he wrote in 'The Three Monuments' with some
bitterness after his speech:

> And all the popular statesmen say
> That purity built up the State
> And after kept it from decay;
> Admonish us to cling to that
> And let all base ambition be,
> For intellect would make us proud
> And pride bring in impurity;
> The three old rascals laugh aloud.

A. N. Jeffares, *W. B. Yeats: Man and Poet*, 1949

The GPO and Nelson Pillar

Nelson and his pillar have gone from the street since the mid-1960s, the first token victim of the imbecilic destruction that for ten years now has harrowed the North. But he was happy up there in 1944 when I was writing:

The traffic moves north and south and east and west, over the Liffey and along the shabby, coloured quays, through crowded streets where Georgian grace has decayed into ragged, smelly slums: and hilly alleys where the mind can remember Dublin of the Danes: around statues – Parnell, and the Capuchin, Father Mathew, and Moore and Burke and Goldsmith and Grattan: and Patrick Sheehan, the policeman who once held a bull by the horns and who lost his life in a sewer when trying to rescue another man . . . The traffic of life burrows through Dublin as mice burrow through a chest of meal: and since Dublin, like all old European cities, has its layers of memories, the mind can burrow backwards through Dublin of the Danes, the Normans, of the eighteenth century, of rebels and writers, of James Joyce and Matt Talbot and Daniel O'Connell and Lady Morgan and Luke Gardiner who, you might say, made the place, and Gogarty and Yeats and a myriad others: and Sean Tracy who was shot dead in Talbot Street and Patrick Pearse who commanded in the Post Office for a few flaming days.

The present is moving here and the past is never dead: and if you stood long enough in O'Connell Street between the Pillar and the Post Office you would come to understand Ireland that is and Ireland that was, all Ireland from Donegal to Wexford, from Antrim to Kerry.

There is Parnell, and the Sacred Heart of Jesus, and Father Theobald Mathew, the Apostle of Temperance. There was Nelson. There is now James Larkin, in Oisín Kelly's splendid statue. There is Sir John Grey of the Freeman's Journal and Vartry Waterworks, to whom all Dubliners who wash themselves and put water in their whiskey owe a lot. There is the gentlemanly revolutionary of 1848, William Smith O'Brien, and there is Daniel O'Connell and his symbolic, surrounding angels.

British army snipers in 1916 shot the angels in their ample bosoms, and not so long ago the Orangemen, following in the exemplary footsteps of the Provisional town-planners, tried to blow them up. What had they got against angels? Or was it the Orangemen? Or the Provisionals? Nobody claimed what those moles oddly call responsibility!

On the far shore of Anna Livia Plurabelle there is Thomas Moore and Thomas Davis and Henry Grattan, orating, and Edmund Burke, meditating, and Oliver Goldsmith reading a book and 'deliberately sipping at the honey-pot of his mind'.

Jim Larkin, the great labour leader, is no stranger to O'Connell Street and his statue stands, arms aloft, as he himself once stood. He is best remembered by James Plunkett in his novel Strumpet City, *and in his Abbey Theatre play,* The Risen People. *The title of the novel*

Plunkett took from Denis Johnston's play, The Old Lady
Says 'No!' *From this passage :*

SPEAKER. Shall we sit down together for a while?
Here on the hillside where we can look down on the
city . . .

> Strumpet city in the sunset
> So old, so sick with memories,
> Old Mother;
> Some they say are damned
> But you, I know, will walk the streets of Paradise
> Head high, and unashamed.

TO THE MASTERS OF DUBLIN: 6 OCT. 1913
(In an open letter to the Editor, *Irish Times*.)

Sirs, I address this warning to you, the aristocracy
of industry in this city, because, like all aristocracies,
you tend to grow blind in long authority, and to be
unaware that you and your class and its every action are
being considered and judged day by day by those who
have power to shake or overturn the whole social order,
and whose restlessness in poverty today is making our
industrial civilization stir like a quaking bog . . .

You do not seem to read history so as to learn its
lessons. That you are an uncultivated class was
obvious from recent utterances of some of you upon
art. That you are incompetent men in the sphere in
which you arrogate imperial powers is certain, because
for many years, long before the present uprising of
labour, your enterprises have been dwindling in the
regard of investors, and this while you have carried
them on in the cheapest labour market in these islands,
with a labour reserve always hungry and ready to
accept any pittance . . .

Those who have economic power have civic power
also, yet you have not used the power that was yours to
right what was wrong in the evil administration of this

city. You have allowed the poor to be herded together so that one thinks of certain places in Dublin as of a pestilence . . .

You may succeed in your policy and ensure your own damnation by your victory. The men whose manhood you have broken will loathe you, and will always be brooding and scheming to strike a fresh blow. The children will be taught to curse you. The infant being moulded in the womb will have breathed into its starved body the vitality of hate. It is not they – it is you who are the blind Samsons pulling down the pillars of the social order . . .

Under the shadow of Larkin's statue we may well meditate on these words of George Russell (AE), poet, philosopher, painter, organizer of co-operative creameries, rebuking the employers of Dublin during the lock-out of 1913: old agonies, old passions, old greeds, old angers that set the mood for more violence to come . . .

His words had special reference to William Martin Murphy, newspaper owner of the time, and also the master of the Dublin tramways. Changed times now in many ways, in Dublin. You can, it is said, always depend on Coras Iompair Eireann (the Irish Transport Company): if you miss one strike you'll catch the next.

Here at O'Connell Bridge and in the novel The Flying Swans *(1957), by the poet Padraic Colum, the young man Ulick O'Reihill sees for the first time Hogan's great statue of O'Connell, the Liberator:*

His cloak flung back, the massive leader was above. Below were winged figures, quiescent but watchful, with drawn but unbrandished swords. The leader was in a lofty place. And the loftiness was in the faces and attitudes of the resting, watching angels. That was what the sculptor had done: he had changed the massiveness of metal into this loftiness.

The passers-by took no stock in the monument. But Ulick remembered his grandfather's talk about it – how he, Breasal O'Breasal, walked to the Capital through the night and an early morning, going along with other men who filled the roads so that they might be on this street on a Sunday when the leader was set up here. Ulick thought of the crowd ready to cheer for the man they had heard in life, but hushed by the sight of that unspeaking bronze.

Here at the feet of the great demagogue in bronze who, according to Balzac, incarnated a nation, we can lean on the bridge and look at the dark and dirty water and bid farewell to the city.

So much we have missed, so much we have forgotten.

Upstream are the Four Courts, downstream the Custom House, the glory of Gandon and the eighteenth century. Here beside us is Bachelor's Walk, and another Anglo-Irish tragedy, and the memory of a painting by Jack Butler Yeats.

Have we forgotten Oscar Wilde in Westland Row and Merrion Square : and his father and mother before him? But then he was a Londoner, and deliberately so, and never a Dubliner. Have we forgotten Sheridan le Fanu and his ghosts, and Maturin, who was maternal uncle to Wilde, and his demoniacal Melmoth the Wanderer, and Sebastian Melmoth dying, beyond his means in Paris; and Tom Moore walking from Aungier Street to Trinity College, and Robert Emmet and Wolfe Tone and Edward Fitzgerald and 'all that delirium of the brave' ; and Sir Philip Crampton, and Samuel Lover, over there in D'Olier Street; and Jimmy O'Dea and Alfie Byrne and the old Theatre Royal, and the Gaiety and the Olympia ; and a thousand others?

May the dark and dirty river, the origin of it all, forgive us for all our sins of omission.

Go against it, upstream to its pure origin above Calary Bog and under the butt of Kippure mountain: follow the river all the way down and round, and under the guidance of one of the greatest of Dubliners, James Joyce, to this dark, final, flowing moment:

Can't hear with the waters of. The chittering waters of. Flittering bats, field mice bawk talk. Ho! Are you not gone ahome? What Thom Malone? Can't hear with bawk of bats, all thim liffeying waters of. Ho, talk save us! My foos won't moos. I feel as old as yonder elm. A tale told of Shaun or Shem? All Livia's daughtersons. Dark hawks hear us. Night! Night! My ho head falls. I feel as heavy as yonder stone. Tell me of John or Shaun? Who were Shem or Shaun the living sons or daughters of? Night now? Tell me, tell me, tell me, elm! Night night! Tell me tale of stem or stone. Beside the rivering waters of hitherandthithering waters of. Night!

James Joyce, *Finnegans Wake*, 1939

'Anna Liffey'

Acknowledgements

The editor and publishers gratefully acknowledge permission to use copyright material in this book:

Brendan Behan: extract from *The Big House* from *The Complete Plays* (Methuen, 1978). Copyright © 1961 by Evergreen Review. Reprinted by permission of Evergreen Review as copyright holder, Methuen, London as publisher, and of Tessa Sayle, Literary Agent.

Joseph Campbell: 'As I walked down through Dublin city' from *The Poems of Joseph Campbell*, edited and with an introduction by Austin Clarke (Allen Figgis & Co., Ltd, 1963).

Austin Clarke: 'No bells rang in her house . . .' from *Too Great a Vine* (Dolmen Press, 1957), and extract from *Irish Writing*, 1957 (editor Sean J. White). Both reprinted by permission of Mrs Nora Clarke.

Padraic Colum: from *The Flying Swans* (1957). Reprinted by permission of Allen Figgis & Co., Ltd.

Tom Corkery's Dublin: extract reprinted by permission of Anvil Books.

Maurice Craig: from *Dublin 1660–1860 : A Social and Architectural History* (1969). Reprinted by permission of Allen Figgis & Co., Ltd.

Robert Farren: 'If the flowers in the Peoples' Gardens . . .' from *Rime, Gentlemen, Please* (Sheed & Ward, 1945). Reprinted by permission of the author.

Oliver St John Gogarty: from 'Ringsend' in *The Collected Poems of Oliver St John Gogarty*. Copyright © 1954 by the Devin Adair Company. Reprinted by permission of Oliver D. Gogarty, and of Devin Adair Co., Inc.

A. Norman Jeffares: from *W. B. Yeats : Man and Poet* (2/e 1962). Reprinted by permission of Routledge & Kegan Paul Ltd.

Denis Johnston: from *The Old Lady Says 'No!'*. Reprinted by permission of Colin Smythe Ltd, Publishers.

James Joyce: from *The Letters of James Joyce*, I, edited by Stuart Gilbert. Reprinted by permission of Faber & Faber Ltd, and Viking Penguin Inc. From *A Portrait of the Artist as a Young Man*. Copyright 1916 by B. W. Huebsch. Copyright renewed 1944 by Nora Joyce. Definitive text Copyright © 1964 by the Estate of James Joyce. Reprinted by permission of Jonathan Cape Ltd, The Society of Authors as the Literary Representative of the Estate of James Joyce, and Viking Penguin Inc. From *Finnegans Wake*. Copyright 1939 by James Joyce, copyright renewed 1967 by George Joyce and Lucia Joyce. Reprinted by permission of The Society of Authors as the Literary Representative of the Estate of James Joyce, and Viking Penguin Inc.

Weston St John Joyce: from *The Neighbourhood of Dublin*. Reprinted by permission of Gill & Macmillan Ltd, Dublin.

ACKNOWLEDGEMENTS

Patrick Kavanagh: 'If ever you go to Dublin town . . .' from *Collected Poems* (2/e, rev., 1972). Reprinted by permission of Mrs Katherine Kavanagh and Martin Brian O'Keeffe Ltd.

George A. Little: from *Malachi Horan Remembers* (Gill, 1943). Reprinted by permission of Gill & Macmillan Ltd.

Christine, Lady Longford: from *Enter Certain Players: Edward Mac Liammoir and the Gate (1928–1978)*, ed. Peter Luke (Dolmen Press, 1978).

Muriel McCarthy: from *All Graduates and Gentlemen: Marsh's Library*. Reprinted by permission of O'Brien Press.

Donagh MacDonagh: 'Dublin Made Me' from *The Hungry Grass* (1947). Reprinted by permission of Faber & Faber Ltd.

Adrian MacLoughlin: from *Guide to Historic Dublin* (1979). Reprinted by permission of Gill & Macmillan, Ltd, Dublin.

Louis MacNeice: 'Dublin' from *Collected Poems* (Faber, 2/e, rev., 1979). Reprinted by permission of David Higham Associates Ltd.

Ria Mooney: from 'The Autobiography of Ria Mooney', published in separate parts in *George Spelvin's Theatre Book* (Proscenium Press).

Flann O'Brien: extract from 'I am a roving sporting blade . . .' and prose extract, both from *At Swim-Two-Birds* (MacGibbon & Kee, 1960/Walker & Co., Inc., 1966). Reprinted by permission of Granada Publishing Ltd, and Walker & Co., Inc.

Sean O'Casey: from *Pictures in the Hallway*, Vol. 2. Reprinted by permission of Macmillan, London and Basingstoke and of John Cushman Associates, Inc.

Frank O'Connor: from *Leinster, Munster and Connaacht* (ed. B. V. Fitzgerald, Hale, 1950). Reprinted by permission of A. D. Peters & Co., Ltd.

Ulick O'Connor: from *Oliver St John Gogarty: A Poet and his Times*. Reprinted by permission of Granada Publishing Ltd.

Gerry O'Flaherty: from an article in *Ireland of the Welcomes*, Jan./Feb. 1975. Reprinted courtesy of the Editor.

Dominic O'Riordan: 'No young Michael Angelo, he, . . .'. Reprinted by permission of Anthony O'Riordan.

Maurice O'Sullivan: from *Twenty Years A-Growing*. Reprinted by permission of the Author's Literary Estate and Chatto & Windus Ltd.

James Stephens: from *The Insurrection in Dublin*. Reprinted by permission of The Society of Authors on behalf of the copyright owner, Mrs Iris Wise.

W. B. Yeats: extract from 'Easter 1916', copyright 1924 by Macmillan Publishing Co., Inc., renewed 1952 by Bertha Georgie Yeats; 'Municipal Gallery Revisited', copyright 1940 by Georgie Yeats, renewed 1968 by Bertha Georgie Yeats, Michael Butler Yeats and Anne Yeats; 'Swift's Epitaph', copyright 1933 by Macmillan Publishing Co., Inc., renewed 1961 by Bertha Georgie Yeats; 'And all the popular statesmen say . . .', copyright 1928 by Macmillan Publishing Co., Inc., renewed 1956 by Georgie Yeats (quoted in A. N. Jeffares, *W. B. Yeats: Man and Poet*). All in *Collected Poems of W. B. Yeats* (2/e Macmillan, London 1950/New York 1956). Reprinted by permission of M. B. Yeats, Anne Yeats and Macmillan, London Ltd, and of Macmillan Publ. Co., Inc., New York.

ACKNOWLEDGEMENTS

While every effort has been made to secure permission we may have failed in a few cases to trace the copyright holder. We apologize for any apparent negligence.

The illustrations in this book were taken from the following sources: Samuel A. Ossory Fitzpatrick, *Dublin* (London, 1907); S. Reynolds Hole, *A Little Tour in Ireland* (London, 1892); Weston St John Joyce, *The Neighbourhood of Dublin* (Dublin, 1912); E. R. McClintock-Dix, *A New Song called Anna Liffey* (Dundrum, 1907); *A Book of Dublin* (Dublin, 1929); Guinness Museum Archive; National Library of Ireland.

Index

MacDonagh, Thomas, 7, 64–5
MacLoughlin, Adrian, 34–6,
 65
MacManus, Francis, 4
MacManus, M. J., 43
MacNeice, Louis, 8–11
Mahony, Francis Sylvester
 ('Father Prout'), 53–4
Mangan, James Clarence, 25
Markiewicz, Constance, 25
Marsh, Narcissus, 35–41
McCarthy, Dr Muriel, v,
 36–7, 41
Montague, John, 58
Mooney, Ria, 98–100
Moore, George, 15–16
Moran, Michael, 65–7
Mulligan, Biddy, 47
Murphy, William Martin, 106

Newman, John Henry, 22–3

O'Brien, Flann, 23–5, 27–9,
 56–8
O'Casey, Seán, 100–1
O'Connor, Frank, 62–3
O'Connor, Ulick, 78–9, 84–6
O'Dea, Jimmy, 47
O'Donoghue, David J., 29–30
O'Donovan, Harry, 47
O'Donovan, John, 53–4
O'Flaherty, Gerry, 1–3
O'Grady, Hugh Art, 84
O'Grady, Standish James,
 83–4

O'Riordan, Dominic, 81–3
Ormonde, Duke of, 13–14
O'Sullivan, Maurice, 33–4

Pearse, P. H., 7
Plunkett, James, 104–5
Pope, Alexander, 42

Robinson, Lennox, 64
Russell, George, 105–6
Ryan, John, 91–2

Shaw, George Bernard, 63–4,
 65
Smyllie, R. M., 43
Sparling, H. Halliday, 87
Spenser, Edmund, 3–4, 48
Stephens, James, 17–18
Swift, Jonathan, 37–40, 41–2
Synge, John, 92–3

Talbot, Matt, 4
Thackeray, William
 Makepeace, 54–5
Tone, Theobald Wolfe, 17

Walsh, John Edward, 49–51
Whaley, Buck, 19
White, Sean J., 60

Yeats, William Butler, 7, 26,
 29, 40, 43, 65–7, 95–7, 101,
 102